THE NORTH STONE REVIEW

NUMBER 13

2001

The North Stone Review is published periodically. Unsolicited manuscripts must include S.A.S.E. – a self-addressed, stamped envelope – as must queries for proposed review-articles, essays or art work. Manuscripts mailed from outside the United States must bear International Reply Coupons for the correct amount of postage. All queries must also bear SASE or they will not be answered.

Subscription rates: $25 for two issues, including postage.

Address: The Editors
The North Stone Review
Box 14098
Minneapolis, MN
55414-0098
U.S.A.
NorthStone@aol.com

Back issues may be ordered via reproduction from Xerox University Microfilms, 300 North Zeeb Road, Ann Arbor, MI 48106. Distribution nationally by Bernhard De Boer, Inc., 113 East Centre St., Nutley, NJ 07110 (973-667-9300) and in the Twin Cities by Don Olson Distribution, 2645-16th Ave. S., Minneapolis, MN 55407 (612-724-2976). / The cover drawing apropos of Julia Budenz's poem sequence is by Louise Viste-Ross.

TABLE OF CONTENTS

7 .... Barry Casselman .... two poems
9 .... Nathan Viste-Ross .... five poems
13 .... Philip Waterhouse .... one poem
14 .... Rebecca Aronson ....one poem
17 .... James Naiden, Louise Viste-Ross
& James Ashe .... collaborative poem
18 .... Susan Wells .... three poems
24 .... Marc J. Sheehan .... one poem
25 .... Tracy Youngblom .... two poems
27 .... Sigrid Bergie .... one poem
28 .... Louise Viste-Ross .... drawing
29 .... Robin Raygor .... fiction
(*The Fish*)
33 .... Jane Whitledge .... three poems
36 .... Mary Pogge .... three poems
40 .... Thomas R. Smith .... five poems
47 .... Robert Joe Stout .... one poem
48 .... Madelon Sprengnether .... two poems
50 .... Robert Bly .... two poems
52 .... David Ignatow .... four poems
56 .... Kathryn Krishna .... two poems
58 .... Paul Ramsey .... two poems
59 .... Daniela Gioseffi .... one poem
60 .... Marvin Bell .... three poems
67 .... Marjorie Buettner .... three poems
69 .... John Daniel .... three poems
74 .... Ruth Stone .... five poems
78 .... Timothy Hodor .... two poems
79 .... Lee Larcomb .... three poems
83 .... Leslie Adrienne Miller .... one poem
86 .... Jonathan Sisson .... six poems
92 .... Calvin Forbes .... two poems
94, 104 .... Louise Viste-Ross .... drawings
95, 105 .... Julia Budenz .... poem sequences
(*Times With the Tease In*
and *Bounds That Let Breeze In*)

124 .... Joe Paddock .... two poems
128 .... Robert Battin. .... drawing
129 .... Robert Bly .... essay
(*On Edna St. Vincent Millay*)
131 .... Nils Peterson .... one poem
132 .... James Longstaff .... two poems
134 .... Gerard Malanga .... three poems
141 .... Jane Spiro .... one poem
143 .... Ralph J. Mills, Jr .... two poems
145 .... Jim Stevens .... one poem
147 .... Chet Corey .... five poems
154 .... Nancy Frederiksen. .... one poem
155 .... Nickie J. Gunstrom .... one poem
156 .... David Culver .... drawing
157 .... Chester G. Anderson .... fiction
(*Right On Down*)
164 .... Robley Wilson .... one poem
165 .... Allen Hamilton Bates .... three poems
168 .... George T. Wright .... two poems
170 .... Maura Stanton .... two poems
174 .... Dennis Saleh .... four prose poems
177 .... Susan McLean. .... four poems
180 .... Charles Edward Eaton .... one poem
181 .... Thomas McCarthy .... three poems
184 .... Jared Carter. .... one poem
185 .... George Roberts .... three prose poems
188 .... Steven Stromme .... six haiku
190 .... Kate Hallett Dayton .... one prose poem
191 .... Karla Hammond .... two poems
193 .... W. R. Moses .... three poems
196 .... Robert Couteau .... one poem
197 .... Baron Wormser. .... three poems
202 .... Alison McGhee .... one poem
203 .... John Mitchell .... one poem
205 .... Susan Yuzna .... one poem
206 .... John Calvin Rezmerski .... two poems

208 .... Freya Manfred .... two poems
210 .... Richard Lyons .... one poem
212 .... Dave Etter .... two poems
214 .... Ethna McKiernan .... two poems
216 .... Hugh Fox .... three poems
219 .... Archibald Henderson .... five poems
224 .... Dara Wier .... one poem
227 .... Steven Tarlow .... one poem
230 .... William Heyen .... three poems
234 .... Melanie Richards .... two poems
235 .... Richard Carr. .... one poem
236 .... Roland Flint .... four poems
241 .... Jean Valentine .... one poem
242 .... Donald Junkins .... three poems
244 .... Glenna Luschei .... two poems
247 .... Kevin Bezner .... one poem
248 .... Eamon Grennan .... one poem
250 .... Michael Moos .... four poems
253 .... William Hathaway .... one poem
254 .... Louise Viste-Ross .... drawing
255 .... James Ashe .... fiction
(*Rain*)
257 .... Saudamini Siegrist .... three poems
260 .... Clark Coolidge .... three poems
263 .... Charlotte Otten .... one poem
264 .... Clarence Major .... two poems
266 .... Carol Ellis .... review-article
(*History And Renaissance: Marvin Bell*)
273 .... John Daniel .... review-article
(*Eden, Goats, Rome, and Voices of Long Ago*)
280 .... .John Daniel. .... review-article
(*Loon Territory*)
286 .... John Daniel .... review-article
(*Six Poets*)
296 .... John Daniel .... review-article
(*The Muse of Eugene J. McCarthy*)

299 .... Dina Ben-Lev .... review-article
(*Leslie Adrienne Miller's Second Book of Poems*)
301 .... Camille D'Ambrose .... review-article
(*A Nation Of Watchers*)
306 .... Camille D'Ambrose .... review-article
(*Indigenous Voices*)
309 .... Jonathan Sisson .... review-article
(*Silent Over Africa*)
318 .... Richard Holinger .... review-article
(*Rewards And Transformations*)
321 .... Robert Lacy .... review-article
(*Two Memoirs, One Journal*)
325 .... Marjorie Buettner .... review-article
(*Four Books of Poems*)
333 .... Michael Fedo .... review-article
(*Emily Carter's Stories*)
335 .... James Naiden .... review-article
(*On Michael Dennis Browne*)
344 .... J. R. Naiden .... review-article
(*Obsequiosness as an Art*)
345 .... The Editor .... Brief Mentions
(*Notices of new books by Alison McGhee, Richard Wilbur, Leslie Adrienne Miller, Michael Fedo, Robert Lacy, Olga Andreyev Carlisle*)
352 .... NOTES ON CONTRIBUTORS

BARRY CASSELMAN

A FOLIAGE PUZZLE

Certain melodies go directly to my agitation,
the routes in my body where there are no illusions,
only sensations accumulated in dispositions,
inclinations, and topologies.

We do mostly a subtle rearrangement.
Our adding is really a kind of subtracting,
since we do not seem to create anything ourselves.
Our adding is taking from something else
before putting it down.
Does the true weight of it actually change?

And our subtracting is really a kind of adding,
since we do not seem to eradicate anything ourselves.
Our subtracting is increasing something else
after taking it away,
after putting it down,
after settling it.

We do subtle rearrangements,
but we are not subtle with each other.

Only the slender aromas of spring flowers are
assurances
while they linger in an almost windless place,
under a huddle of streets,
with puzzles of sunlight reflected here and there
on foliage.

I don't know why you are here.

SINECURE

Shout, sing songs riding in the car,
at bad moments I play Schubert in my ear,
perhaps a maneuver, abstaining
from the noise war.

My head is turned easily,
the baroque flute, clarinets,
permutations in tones,
commandos of trumpets.

But the sounds playing in my own head are better.

Noises attach themselves,
I spend a legacy in darkness,
sedans, lakes at dawn.

NATHAN VISTE-ROSS

AN ITINERANT OBSERVATION

In a green-yellow growing field, a
Dirt-walled stonehouse
Grows to unrelieving proportions –

The rain etches lifeprints
on the outside four forewalls.
Four highways in two crosses
each run on to ending:
Another dirt stonehouse,
standing alone.
One brown river with blue tendrils
passes through each still dwelling;
Lightens the muddamp with sweet taste,
taste unknown.
Inside the protection
of the crumbling, bland shelter,
a niche of soft men
flame a candle unseen:
But the air, thick and silky,
supports only embers
that eat the fuel slowly;
And the rich virgin wax
turns to quivering ash
and a glow, barely lean.

KEEPING UP APPEARANCES

All of the speakers played all of the instruments;
All the audience wept.
Out of proportion to anything concert,
Sonorities bent.
The podium angled an arc toward the crowd;
Along the rows the response waved, thrust,
Pushed off endurance;
From rear, rose a statue: fatigued the event.

Pushing a hard smooth from up the marble plain;
— rising through, rising through —
Crack! Relief from form, and ah,
Pull the, to unwilling view, the
Everlonging lyric rise t' reach too far.
— the sepulcher pushed past from out the stone malaise —
The smooth platter-shatter should
Tell to reach:

Another tell to concert sing a song of hope, reach, bonding ring?
We won't want!
Another sleek plateau; at best: statue rubble beauty;
Once harmony, but now not.
— going by, going by; all be'ng 's too told —
Day are dreams; play these throngs.
Play our, all abreast, relieving pride.

POUSEE-CAFÉ

Each time the waitress walked by —

The frond in the pressed-glass flask
On the table in the shadow-torn room
In the inn in the cool suburban town
Quivered lightly.

He liked the feel of the sound of the people
Talking 'round him;
Whisp'ring egos as ballet;
A chaos, ordered only by a dream.

And the shadows overlapped
And the egos overlapped
And the whispers overlapped
And the shadows of the egos in the whispers
Told the dream.

And the man at the table in the inn in the town
Dreamt himself in dance with the people.

PIDGINS

Dove's dreams roll, fly by, past my days;
fluttering.
Withdrawn time tells me my flights should
part the dawn.
Eached arched path, in approach, songs
the dove's morning;
Must seek the dove's flightflow, rescue
the doved warning.

UNLOADING PERFUME

Chattertales buzz through the walkie-talkie,
Punctuate the drone of the forklift's humm.
Conveyors convolute to a daylight destination
And their clatter off the concrete carves a cavernous
  metronome.
In an upright, agile arc, she deftly slides a ton
Of capsuled, lilac liquid into the vast, steel comb.
Rattle-lifted open, a corrugated door
Bleeds a patch of brilliant into the sodium lamp cones.
A tractor plugs the hole with a box of fragrant colluvium.
She scoops a stack from the trailer's mouth
On the fork of her iron beast;
And in through the air, in a swing to the comb,
Plants the gelatinous, creaking load.
The cave shudders from the thud of the beast
As she rams it on into another container
Of freight to colonnade in her warehouse.

PHILIP WATERHOUSE

LEADFOOT

Another poem is back,
rejection slip the printed kind.
The editor added handwritten comment:
I should use a more even strike
on the old manual, make it easier on the old
editing eyes.
Always grateful for the personal touch.

My favorite piano teacher
was like that, said my jerky groping
for the right note made her feel like she
was sliding off the end of the bench,
and left an encouraging message:
Good luck with your next instructor.

I didn't have, nor with the one after,
ad nauseum.
But I was impressed just the same how
nice they all were when they came to their
stops, too.

Remembering makes me
want to work harder, not get down
on myself, keep putting the old poems in
the mail. Hit the right note.

I would not have wanted to be any
of them trying to teach me how to play the piano.

REBECCA ARONSON

SPEAKING IN TONGUES

I

I am breathing clouds
onto a dark window,
tracing letters among them
with one cold finger.
The words of everyone before me
float loose in my blood — it is why
I always have something to say.
Some of the words rest low like shadows
waiting in case I grow
into their use. I don't yet know them
by sound. Some arrive before I am ready,
I form the shapes but don't know
their order. Through language
we honor what is ours: the stories
and places, the terrible
beautiful dead. We tell what we must,
inevitably, with or without
the necessary words.
On the window I etch unfamiliar letters,
new codes I cannot decipher.
We tell what we must remember.
On the window the hieroglyphs blur
and fade, when I am ready to read them
I have only to breathe.

II

Grandmother grew up
speaking German, rejected it
as soon as she could.
Never taught
her children any stories
that needed those words
for their telling. If you are silent
does that mean you have forgotten
what you know?
Like trees we shed our leaves
sometimes to prepare
for another season. She
dropped memories around her
while we tried to gather
the scattered stories.

Her last words
crackled and were bright
with sounds it was too late
for us to learn.

III

In the first snow we shuffle and leap,
throw ourselves forward to form messages
that are best read from a distance.
What we have in mind are birds,
low flying jets, anyone
from another world. What we will settle for
is the slow deciphering of our names
before a wind sends drifts
across our day's work.
Someone returning home
might read the names looped
along the side of the small hill,
tell a story over dinner
to a listening family
and somehow they will know us, and somehow
our stories will become theirs.

SECOND CHANCE

Waiting for swordfish on the grill
Reverberates to the front steps.
And waiting forever with the sand's white ash.
Flesh pressed, sweat and too many bright lights.

1 June 1996
Minneapolis

SUSAN WELLS

BABY TEETH

I found your baby teeth
wrapped in plastic next to
the leather boxes of moonstones
from agate beach next to the
old watch band hooks and eyes
and the knitted puppets
with orange hair

I thought of mothers putting
baby teeth in their pockets
going to look at long lines
of daughters in a park somewhere
mothers of grown daughters
shaking the little teeth in
their pockets singing softly

(in my case the wadaleecha
song) signing in at the entrance
to the park sheila mother of
carol ann mina mother of jean

but all the daughters would
have changed their faces so
as not to be recognized a mole
or a birthmark moved to another
knee dimples removed eyebrows
stylishly thinned

to be finally free of their
mothers all identifying marks
would have been removed

at first I might have cried
shown my handful of teeth but
what a relief to throw them up
see them change into sparkles of
blue and white over the line
of girls you can't know how sharp
those little points can be
how they dug into my hand

MACHINE GUN POETS FROM LOS ANGELES

I will listen to
machine gun poets from
Los Angeles
only so long.

passing up microphones they
stand on the edge of a
white stageblue lights
feet pointed in,

young and
not so young
machine gun poets doing a
word blast four nights
before Halloween in
Venice, California.

I will lean forward
into the blue lights
only so long,
watching them burn,
glass volleys from a
boy's mouth missing my neck,
catching me in the arm,
grazing a breast,
drawing blood,

talking about
crimes against the earth,
crimes against children,
hit and run governments,
family secrets.

look at me here. Tall,
long-waisted woman, mouth
like a boy, mouth like a
long O, sixth row on the end.
look at me timing myself,
look at me knee to knee
with the machine gun poets of
Los Angeles, watching their
thin elbows slicing the air,
time-keepers breathing out
"you" and "ho", "yo" and "ho",

only so long before I
lift my green skirt,
look at me lifting my
long green skirt, softly
wiping the faces of
machine gun poets
from Los Angeles.

WATER LIKE THIS

I see how those women before me,
those aunts in flowered aprons who
moved from one meal to the next
in their best grace, that view of

birch trees from the front window,
delicate in every season, men
in easy chairs with ottomans
picking through pipe tobacco,

and in the thinning evening light,
that old grandfather, sponging
himself with a shaking hand, the
bathroom door ajar. I see now

the more serious aunt, her
swollen hands in rubber gloves
from too much washing, lead me to
the kitchen sink as an altar,

hopeful for a star pupil to
emerge, but over and over again
I failed her, wasting water.
my heart was never in it.

things like this hold in my body
now: a tall cousin playing waltzing
matilda on his accordion, his
mother's cloth napkin on his knee.

it was my aim to get him in the
closet after meals, to nudge him
into something with my tongue, but
his was a dry cool mouth. He could not

guide me through those watery ways,
and down in the mud-bottomed lake,
I pulled my flat-chested mother (in
whose heart sang dragonflies and

wild dogs) farther and farther from the
shore, where aunts, humming their way
through daisy chains and mah jong, exclaimed
"oh that young skin, that young skin."

MARC J. SHEEHAN

FROM DUST

Here the flat land
is patchy with ground water,
earth-clouds that moles fly through.

Here even the apples in the abandoned
orchard
are knobbed and creased as potatoes,
blind in all their eyes,
lacking only starch.

Here you could spade the garden mounds
and unearth a mole.
Picking it up you'd feel the pink
star of its nose rooting
through the intricate clay of your fingers.

TRACY YOUNGBLOM

SECRETS OF THE BOWL

If we did our math, we thought
we could solve her – elbows

angled out, stick
straight spine, ridiculous small

orb of a head. All her lines
and points bent around her

work, her body a barrier.
She stirred, intentional

circles, secrets of the bowl,
her cakes and cookies turned

out on the table. Summers
she stacked the freezer full,

nothing mattered except eggs,
shortening, the flour sifted down,

its veil of perfection. Her floury
cheeks runneled, the formal

presentation of her back.
All the forms of her hands: opening

to rub a stomach in bed, clenched
around coffee, cupping a face. We

walked shapes around her, found no
access, her circumference impermeable,

took refuge in her corners, sharp
with mystery, waited long days

for a key to the cache in her
hollow bones.

MEN AND WOMEN

At first the alignment
was perfect; kissing

was great, sex
juicy, two halves of fleshy

peach clinging
together, um-hm.

Then something shifted
on account of desire,

he grew taller or she
grew shorter, nothing

matched up. Now
he reaches for her cheek

in the impossible space
above her head

while she longs for his voice
but sees only his throat,

stark bony knuckle sliding
up and down.

SIGRID BERGIE

FACE OF MY EYE

my eye the pole of a merry-go-
round resurrecting streaks of
wind-whipped grass   the cars
sail round and round in
geometric screeches   the trees
are softer velocity in flowing
complex gestures the houses
mainly sit, certain but polite
in their movements   human arms
and legs transmit their bodies
like skilled tight-rope walkers
along the horizontal planes
higher than an airplane, fingers
of clouds buttress the sky nylon,
projecting their full grip beyond
my eyeball, its lens dimmed in
this multi-earth decor defying
the mind's gravity
my eyelid stretches in primal attack
over the labyrinthine eye

THE FISH

By Robin Raygor

I guess I'm just not very flexible. Jack always said that about me. Maybe that's why he left me. I don't know; maybe I'm just not cut out to live under water. It's so wet and dark. I remember I used to think Boston was kind of damp. If it rained two or three days in a row I'd get all depressed and tell Jack I wanted to move to the desert. He'd say "This is nothing. Wait till we move underwater."

At first I thought he was kidding. I mean, who'd want to live underwater? Then he started bringing home all these books on things like marine biology and aquaculture and he'd talk for hours about mollusks and seaweed. I thought it was kind of a fantasy like some men think of moving to a farm or building a cabin in the wilderness and living on nuts and berries. Jack's fantasy was always the same: he wanted to live under water. I think it was his name that got him to thinking about this stuff. His parents had some sense of humor. I guess you had to with a name like Fish. "Jumpin' Jack Fish" the kids used to call him when he was in school. He was always saying "At least they didn't name me 'Tuna.'"

We kind of had a fight about the twins when they were born. He wanted to call them "Jackson" and "Pollock" but he didn't really press it. I said we should give them the most normal names we could think of to make up for their last name. We ended up with "James" and "Michael." Even so, I've always felt like we had something to make up to them.

During the summer before it was time for the twins to start first grade, I said I should go school shopping for them. Jack said it was a waste because by fall we'd be in the ocean. I didn't know what to think but I've always had a hard time arguing with Jack. It turned out he was right.

One morning toward the end of August I was pouring Jack's coffee and I noticed he was kind of agitated. He kept rubbing his knees with his hands and looking all around the room.

"Well," he said, "this is the day."

"What day?" I was trying to think. Was it somebody's birthday?

"The day we move to the ocean," Jack said.

Of course then I thought he meant he had rented a beach house or something. I never really took the underwater talk too seriously.

He wouldn't tell me where we were going and when I tried to pack, he kept telling me I wouldn't need things. He kept talking about "the sea's infinite bounty" or something like that. He wouldn't let me bring my matchbook collection or TV Guide or any electrical appliances. He piled all of us into the Volvo and started driving like he did when I was pregnant and he was taking me to the hospital. I kept asking him to slow down but it was no use.

It took us about three days to get to Key West. Jack had circles under his eyes but he was still excited. He stopped at the first beach we came to and made us all walk down to the water. The twins were looking up at me to see if everything was all right. I tried to stay calm.

It was when Jack started talking about how to breathe underwater that I started really to get worried. On the trip down I had begun to take his fantasy a little more seriously but figured that once we'd put on air tanks and flippers he'd see that this was impractical in the long run. I mean, you couldn't keep coming up to fill your tanks and still expect to make a decent living. (In fact, what would you be doing for a living in the first place?) Now I began to see that he wasn't talking about tanks or air or any of that. He just wanted to walk into the water and live there.

He had me take his hand and we started into the water. The twins were hanging on to my dress and when the water got up to my knees, Mike started to whimper. Jack never slowed down and soon we were all in over our heads. I was fighting for air and so were the twins, but after a few minutes I found I could breathe the water. You had to breathe slower, just as Jack had told us, and it had a kind of sad, salty taste to it like stale crackers, but we didn't pass out or anything. I wondered if someone had pulled us out at that moment if we would have appeared to them as people who had drowned. I still wonder about that sometimes.

The bottom was sandy at first but as we went deeper, it became rocky and we started to see seaweed and coral. The twins became interested in the fish and Jimmy was kind of poking at a sea turtle. Talking was kind of a chore with all that water in your system, but Jack wanted to warn us about things like jellyfish and moray eels. He had told us all this before back in Boston, but we hadn't really been listening.

When we got down deep enough that the sun was just a tiny gold mirror far above us, Jack said we were in our new home. It didn't look like much to me but I thought maybe if we had some curtains and a television — but then I thought, where are those going to come from down here? I hadn't seen any stores on our way down.

After a few days, we settled into a routine. We had found a better spot on the side of a small coral reef. Jack would spend most of the day looking for food and bringing back interesting shells and pieces of coral. At first I tried to run a kind of school for the twins, but talking was so hard, and I didn't have any books or crayons or anything. I felt bad that they never got to have nap time or milk and cookies, but Jack said that mother nature was giving them the best education a kid could have. After I gave up on the school idea, I spent most of my time just resting and trying to keep an eye on the twins.

At first, Jack spent a lot of time showing things to me and the twins. He'd bring back things he found or take us on trips to see interesting coral formations or wrecks on the bottom. The twins always seemed eager to learn new things and I tried to be interested, but I just couldn't. I had trouble traveling anyway because of my dress. Jack and the twins started going naked shortly after we got here but I was never really comfortable with the idea. I fastened clams on the hem of my dress to keep it from floating up around me, but it still gave me trouble unless I moved very slowly. I think Jack was disappointed in me and he started taking just the twins. As they got older, he started going off more and more by himself. He started talking a lot about finding out what was in the bottom of the Marianas Trench, and one day he just didn't come back and we never saw him again. I guess you could say I got the house.

In spite of everything it seems like my life isn't that different from when we were in Boston, although I still miss the television set. Sometimes boats go by far above us and I try to imagine people on them doing things we used to do but the pictures in my head always end up full of fish and seaweed. I tried to take the twins back up on dry land once but they didn't really want to go and anyway I couldn't find the shore. We wandered around for about three days until they finally led me back to our spot on the coral reef.

I don't really mind it now without Jack. The twins have showed me how to get things to eat although I don't really like seafood. Sometimes they're gone for days at a time. I've started a kind of shell collection. I particularly look for shells with small holes near either end. I've got over three hundred shells now.

JANE WHITLEDGE

AT THE WOLF KILL

A dozen ravens scavenge
in a clearing among balsams
where a stain, like ignited tree-shade,
spreads a violent pink on the snow.
Dark wings rise at our approach
as ravens flee to a rim of pines
where they hunch, silhouettes
like so many hieroglyphs. One raven poses
on the far snow: dark ampersand
between us and the landscape.

We come to look, drawn by raven-shrieks,
our snowshoes braiding a path through woods
to this place: remains of a deer, scraps
of hide, ribs; the head and spine intact
like some macabre hobbyhorse, the blank eye-
socket pleading indifference
to the slaughter.

Raven-tracks form a dense crosshatch that
cancels every wolf-print on the packed snow;
they etch a kind of cuneiform, an ancient
alphabet we'd find indecipherable if we tried.
We study the hard snow, faintly
looking for signs other than the obvious ones.
Wolves have already eaten most of the flesh.
Before leaving, we salvage the tongue.

EVERYTHING MUST CHANGE

Now the diligent root slackens
The flies are fat and slow,
and the pallid aster petals
curl among brown bracken.

Gone, too, the summer bird.
The leaf and tendril blacken.
A sigh in the tall dry grass
means: no looking backward —

everything must change or move
or die. Even the ant, bored
into a bed of rotted wood, knows,
but doesn't approve or disapprove.

Now fails the pale corydalis,
and the red death of maples
is done. Ice shuts the frog pond
without malice.

DEPARTURE

And the fish swim in the lake and do not even own clothing.
— Ezra Pound

I shed my clothes on the rock shore
where last summer I watched a snake
slip out of its skin and leave
the husk behind like a discarded sock.
My shirt and jeans, my underthings,
copy that cast-off posture
as I slip into the lake.

On my back I swim away from shore,
away from my accustomed coverings,
and watch a breeze stir an empty cuff,
then lift a collar. My pile of stuff
becomes incidental as the snake-skin
shucked on the rock. I dive deep
and almost imagine never coming back.

MARY POGGE

WRITING FOR RELEASE

slowly one button at a time
I will bare your body as an eraser bares a slate
to words
down the side of your throat
my tongue will write
an opening paragraph punctuated by my teeth
in the skin of your shoulder
across the empty page
of your chest
it will flow
busy as the ink from my pen
below your waistband
my fingertips dance
like they have done
upon the keys of my typewriter
coaxing feeling
with touch
in much the same way
chapter after chapter
writing all night long
I will turn phrases you've never known
opening your eyes wider
when the plot hits its peak
so many twists
so many turns
to reach the climax
until my imagination has dried
and words are left
hanging in the air
until I write
the sequel

PENETRATION

how deep
can you go
with a seven-inch cock
deep enough
to touch my
fingertips
tingle
to choke
the back of my throat
strangle my words
into incoherent
utterings
but never
far enough
to reach my heart

HORMONAL HONEY

I
with my hands laced
across the tidy rounded swell
of my lower belly
I tighten my jaws
clamp against a moan
every month
the moon pulls this pain from me
I cannot help regarding this part
of the mechanical me
as slightly vile
nothing about this
juicy little bodily function
seems sweet

II
two weeks and some later
my belly flat and hard and warm
I tighten my jaws
clamp against a moan
as your tongue traces the sharp contours
of my pelvis
you kiss me with an earthy woodsy cunty smell
light on your lips
your fingers and tongue
finding this part
of the mechanical me
a delicious miracle
this juicy little bodily function
amazingly sweet

III
any quiet private night
in drowsy darkness
I tighten my jaws
clamp against a moan
as my fingers follow
the tidal pull within to quell
an unruly inner riot
of longings and loneliness
this part of the mechanical me
unable to sleep
in the sweet sweet absence of you

THOMAS R. SMITH

ERIC HAMPTON

assaulted February 6, 1995;
taken off life supports February 8, 1995

For days the city's been in shock
over the murder of twenty-eight-
year-old Eric Hampton, his
head kicked in and not
a scratch elsewhere on his body.

Witnesses say the assailants
were black men, maybe walk-in's ("non-
members") at the Y where Hampton
had played basketball earlier
on the evening of his death.

It took me back to one claustro-
phobic night in a small Wisconsin
town in the Sixties, traveling
with a rock band playing at a
nearby club, and how a long-haired

guitar player and I, talking with local
girls, were suddenly mobbed by
boys in leather jackets, one of whom
assaulted my friend: A fist
shot through the open window,

mashed lips against teeth. Blood
dripping onto his satin shirt,
Lon dejectedly agreed to drive
on. Afterward, we both admitted
we'd feared worse, so even my

bloodied friend counted us lucky —
an occupational hazard for rock and
rollers in those days, admired on
stage, but in the street a lightning-
rod for the boys' envy.

So it was with recognition I shuddered
for the trampled face and fled
spirit of Eric Hampton, for whom
the first blow was not a warning
but the piston of death,

though it wasn't until this morning,
driving in the low-rent neighborhood
where I go twice a week to
swim, that, noticing young
black schoolboys trudging through

the snow with their books, it
occurred to me to wonder how they
might see me wrapped in my rusty
Detroit armor, so removed from their
struggle – an unwelcome visitor? –

and imagine them grown men, too
poor to buy a membership at the
Y, striding out on the gym floor
to possess it any way they could,
burning with a wronged brightness.

CUTTING VENISON FOR STEW

The blood has stopped. I spread
the brown slab on a cutting board.
An eye of bone watches me warily.
Raw meat has the weight of necessity.

It's a woven thing, then, flesh –
a strong, joyful, secret weave
that bullets can fray but not
understand. A serrated knife rips seams.

Each remnant carries the scent of
the life – thin oils of winter bark,
sweet grasses of the sun, the tang
of danger at the edge of thickets,

that final giving. Lifting
these breathing garnets into the
skillet, I am putting my hands
in a wounded buck's side.

FROM THE FRANKLIN AVENUE BRIDGE IN MAY

Leaning from the railing, one sees in the currents how much spring costs the Mississippi in uncertainty and turmoil – eddies, fed by melted snow, stir the bottom, a brown stew that boils up suddenly. Thinnings in the clouds cast reflective nimbuses on the swirled coppery metalwork of the river. A railroad trestle's double lies down like a ladder into deep water.

Moist, shadowless air flattens the prospect without haziness, a thin veil interposed between the world and our vision, that tenderness without which, Dostoyevsky said, truth is unjust.

This daylight phosphorescence isn't only the lemony fountains of willows, the feathery stoles of cottonwoods and elms, but the ground itself, the fallen trunks and the secretive folds of dunes, each rock and twig that took the hit of winter. Doesn't every tree climbing up into its rustling, shining garment praise the sun? Praise makes the lace of the chlorophyll fine. Human dances and songs also clothe the angel, drape her in leaves and blossoms of imagination.

RIVERSIDE PARK POEM

1.
Early morning in late October, the sun low in orange mist.
I look across the dew-soaked grass at damp benches.
To the east, rusty, half-shadowed oaks thin toward the Mississippi;
to the west, that street of apartment buildings and duplexes
fronting the park, hippie houses of the Sixties
where a girl sat up all night on methedrine
dripping a Gothic castle of melted candle wax,
where a boy hiding from the FBI had conversations
with a pile of dust on the attic floor,
and where I spent recklessly the spare change of my youth,
panhandled from luck, living by the graces of kind women.

2.
Well, was that all there was to it?
Some days yes; some days no.

3.
These oaks, the oldest trees in Minneapolis,
keep their rust-brown foliage until spring.
I watch a crow settle on one of the highest branches,
spread and shake out its wings – black, angular fans –
then fold them. A second crow arrives, lights on
a neighboring branch a little above the first, fans its wings and
    settles also.
The third, like ash from a forgotten fire,
sifts down among the others. All face
in one direction: toward the river and the fiery mystery opening
again.

4.
What we did with our days, we said, mattered less
than the possibilities we found in them, what we took back
in imagination and desire from our parents' prison.
I can still remember that outlaw faith,
waking under shrubs on a June morning with dew
on my hair and a nickel bag in my pocket, to the braying
of rush hour traffic at a standstill on the river bridge.
I could live on five dollars a week; I knew I would eat,
thanks to someone else's day job, elude the fate of commuters
who once in my altered vision became the colors of their cars.

5.
I did not begrudge the working men and women their living,
remorselessly driving heavy wheels over the earth on their errand of
good or evil.
I can forgive myself the meals never paid back in kind;
we stole like the hands of God stealing from each other.
It wasn't about having things.
It wasn't about building something that would last.
It wasn't about being anyone.
It was about a search
a song that flew that summer on strange black wings through
etherealized bodies.
It was about crows perched together on the highest branches, facing
the sun.

GOODBYE

In the frozen driveway, I shake
my father's hand, a hand
still capable of painful gripping, and bend
to my mother's bird-quick kiss.

Our back seat and trunk are festive
with tattered wrappings of gifts
which, like those we gave, don't come near
saying what no one here will say in words.

But for the time being we must bless them,
for they are now all we have of who we once were
together, each visit a descent, an excavation
for the potsherds of a love that bore us.

We say our goodbyes as fresh snow settles
on trees and rooftops, on gauzy blackberry tents
and on eaves overhanging the dark garage
filled with an odor of animal necessity.

My parents stand well-matched in their
stubbornness, balanced before old age
on the bone-breaking ice. I see
that something in them wants it, this

freezing, if they will not have the fire.

ROBERT JOE STOUT

HE AND I

He rises from the bones of antelope
And whitened buffalo skulls:
My father, young,
Hair swept back
And hands grown into guns.

                                        I run
Towards him and he kneels,
Shooting.
                I spin;
Meadow flowers tangle
My plunge towards daylight,

His voice the wind
From a north that I hear at odd moments
Of silence;
                his face
The flesh I peel each morning
From the bathroom mirror.

MADELON SPRENGNETHER

BRIAR ROSE: THE WISH

Where I was
I could hardly breathe.

Was I unconscious
in a coma

or so sleep-drugged
I looked like death?

You didn't know me then.

Did you dream of me
swimming towards you

through this undertow
of my life?

How my throat ached
for the sibilance

of your name.

How I wished for you
like a new fate.

BRIAR ROSE: THE CHRISTENING

Somehow I was not invited
to the feast

where everyone was joyous
their hands full of gifts.

I should have lived out
my days like them

eating from a golden plate.

Instead, I spit back
my insult

to rid myself
of its carrion taste.

At fifteen, this child
I prophesied

will be cut
to the quick. Let her

exsanguinate.

May she bear
my curse.

ROBERT BLY

READING JAMES WRIGHT

I see ordinary pain
Grow out of your lines
Like hair on the back of hands.
Yours was an orphan
Song. War done,
You drifted on a raft
Like the ocean-people,
Trailed by sharks, sheltered
By one or two palm leaves
Shaped like ears.
You loved poetry more than life,
So you put your elegant
Language skiff back into the brine,
To live or die.

THE CITY OF GOD

We all like poems
That begin with tea,
And end with God.

For example, a man is
Drinking tea and a mouse
Runs across the floor.

It makes him think
Of all hidden things,
A furry cruelty with paws.

It is a secret with ears,
A child of shame, the man thought
He could tell no one of,

Darting and parlaying
His tiny claw-hands among
The sacks of grain, below that awful

Cat of Augustine.

DAVID IGNATOW

A BRIEF BIOGRAPHY

Begin from the vacant.
A room unoccupied
I had forgotten
having left to visit
other rooms elsewhere
in adventure. I am back
in mind to this room.
It contains my childhood
where I sat and listened
to voices of my elders
who sat in leather chairs
and talked.

I listened, enthralled with life
for having induced such stories
I too wanted to tell,
hard, complicated, sometimes funny,
of pith, of magnitude, of accomplishment
and resignation, finally to become
the person seated in such a room
as this to tell the story
and be content that it would come
to telling in a room with others
with whom to share a falling short,
to be constrained to telling.
I listened and was curious
that one could talk of failure
with passion, as if to talk
was in itself success.

I became respectful of speech,
I could expect to speak
with that same authority
as could my elders and learn
to give my troubles my respect
for giving me the means
with which to exercise my satisfaction
in speaking to my peers who then
would speak to me in turn
with equal force of having lived:
a gathering as a child I sat
and listened to: a round of happenings
I learned to care about
in my elders.

I AM ALONE AS I WRITE

yet writing this places me
within the society of others
who, acknowledging it or not,
enact my solitude. But having said
it sets me apart in a silent community
turned in on itself,
away from truth.
We cannot act by truth.
It is not life.

SINCE THEN

I am in search of revival,
entering living rooms,
kitchens and bedrooms
in search of a beginning.

Since then, I have had nothing
to say, inwardly silent,
sun warming me to write:
what I am left to do.

AND I WOULD

Hart Crane a suicide
in mid-ocean and I
at eighteen offered
a job in advertising,
Crane's livelihood.

My father insisting
I earn my living,
if not in his bindery –
I felt it beneath me –
offered this job
through contact
with a friend.

Would I take the job
and find myself
breaking off
as did Crane,
the work humiliating
to him.
In my hand the telephone

number of the firm
I had the name of

and its executive
waiting for my call.
I had the nickel
for the call
placed it
in the slot and
dialed and heard
a voice, his voice
who would hire me.
I believed it was
his voice, and I
saw Crane's body
floating
face down
in mid-ocean, and I
hung up and walked
back to my father's
shop.

I would make my way
through all the hard
things that would
happen to me
there and I would
live defiantly.

1994

KATHRYN KRISHNA

STORM

The satin undersides of leaves
belly themselves to the sky
leaping in the green wind
Feathers and earth powder
from the hens' small dust arroyos
spiral across the drive
aspiring skyward
The hens come crackling and ruffled
stiff-legged run for cover
feathers blown out like petticoats
over their pink frightened skin
I laugh in the wind
turning my face into it
once more
before running on
to latch stable doors

MEMORY

after Edson

A man, not being able to remember
what he wants to remember,
opens up his head and takes everything out
and puts it on the table
Then he cannot remember
why he is in the kitchen
It is a nice day, he says
I will go fishing
While he is gone his wife comes and says
Look at the eels Father caught for dinner
and cooks up every bit with some white wine
How do you like it? she asks
It tastes like something I remember, he says

PAUL RAMSEY

NURSERY RHYME, MODERNIZED

Needles and pins.
Needles and pins.
When a girl marries
Her unmarriage begins.

LOVERS' QUARREL: A METAPHYSICS

When a match is thrown on the water,
It hisses cessation.

When the bow is drawn,
The arrow is still.

They speak their anger
In the silence they will.

DANIELA GIOSEFFI

WAKE ME UP IN A HUNDRED YEARS

when I've grown a green
kelp sea green beard.
Just let me lie here by the sea
in sand beneath
a constant acclamation of wing to wind
currents that carry gulls' cries
as a cormorant cuts the sky
oh, wake me up
in a hundred
years
when
I've
grown a green
kelp sea green beard
among the dunes
of time and sun
among the tunes of seaswept runes
among the dunes of seas and times
among eternal windswept rhymes
among forever singing chimes
after all the human crimes
are done

MARVIN BELL

THE BOOK OF THE DEAD MAN (#40)

1. *About the Dead Man and Desire*

When the dead man itches, he thinks he has picked up a splinter.
Unable to free himself of an itch, the dead man thinks he has a
splinter.
The dead man looks at a praying mantis and sees a pair of twee-
zers.
He offers himself to be walked on by claws.
He waits for the odd fox to trot across his chest and strings of ants
to scrape him pore to pore.
He anticipates the flaying action of chemicals and the sponge baths
of the rain.
The dead man, scoured, is the ruby servant of the vineyard.
The dead man is the salt of the earth, the dust and the sawdust, the
honey in the wine.
Hence, his thoughts must rise to the moon and beyond to take
his mind from that splinter if it is a splinter, that itch if an
itch is what it is.
Everything the dead man thinks has its other side.
The dead man thinks Saturn has been much married but forever
lonely.

2. More About the Dead Man and Desire

If he were just valves and glue, just honey and chocolate, just hot
and cold, the dead man's thoughts would not hop, skip and
jump so.
If he were just comparative, if he were absolute, if he knew his
own mind, the dead man's heart would not race so.
Who but the dead man wonders which of its moons Jupiter favors?
Who knows better than the dead man in his bones the pitch at
which the earth breathes?
The dead man is rapt before the altar of consciousness.
He enters the forbidden realms of experience without penalty.
To the dead man, there is something grave about umbrellas,
something sinister about servitude, something debilitating
about knowledge – like sunlight on slugs.
The dead man rolls back into place the rock that was moved
to find out.
Like Sisyphus, the dead man wants what he has.
When there is no more meek, no vainglorious, no catch-as-
catch-can, no inheritance, no opportunity knocking
that is not also the wind, then naturally the dead man
lives for love.
The dead man, fervent to feel, makes no distinction between
a splinter and a stinger that cost something its life.

THE BOOK OF THE DEAD MAN (#47)

1. *About the Dead Man and Famine*

When the dead man feels pangs, he thinks he is in the Sudan or
Somalia when the crops failed.
Feeling hunger pangs, the dead man thinks he is all bones.
Hollow cheeks give way to no-cheeks, a flat abdomen fills with air.
Witness the dead man fall in, line up, relinquish and shrink.
Was not the dead man taller once, heftier, closer to heaven?
The dead man passes his hands through the shadows of
sagging flesh.
He points a skeletal forefinger at the water carrier and the cook.
He quivers from cold, trembles when the trucks thunder in with
rations.
He pulls himself up by a gossamer thread connected to tomorrow.
He stands in the food line like a construct of bones half hidden by a
dropcloth.
The dead man's stomach no longer rumbles.
Dried-up potions, bags of totemic remains, cosmetic invocations
to universal powers, letters to the authorities now weight
the air – immobile, debilitating artifacts.
The dead man sniffs the air with the last of his lung power.
His chips, shreds and tatters will be the good luck charms of left-
over believers.
The dead man neither believes nor doubts but is nourished by half-
measures.
The dead man is free to go.

2. *More About the Dead Man and Famine*

The dead man's condemnation would be for all time, so he does
not condemn.
The look in the dead man's eyes widens to encompass four food
groups, five grains, seeds and sauces, livestock and prey.
His famine is not a fast.
He rouses himself for a meal, he transforms his geometric figure –
triangles, trapezoids – into the number "1," he jingles and
jangles as if he were a dancer festooned with jewelry, but it
is only the click clacking of loosened tongue and groove.
This is not purgation but the good intentions of the fearful.
Who but the dead man can convey salutes, cheers and accolades to
the starving in Somalia, the Sudan, those living in the erod-
ing landfill from which the good stuff has been taken?
Who better than the dead man to welcome the Malthusians?
When there is no horrifying number, no catastrophe that cannot be
miniaturized, no news too big for a box, no lack more immediate than others, then the dead man does not linger.
The dead man wonders not why but who.
He files the forms that will be found afterwards, he fills in the
blanks that will furnish the data, he obliges by coming
to a full stop.
The dead man wonders not what but when.

THE BOOK OF THE DEAD MAN (#52)

1. *About the Dead Man and Little Much*

High density sunshine adds weight to the dead man's eyelids.
Some say it's the humidity, but it's the heat.
The dead man, watching the surface percolate, charts the seepage.
It's the heat, it's the torpor of the day, it's the high cost of living.
The dead man is waysoever into lifting and living, what with
    pressure bearing down and the rushing about overhead
    to forget.
The dead man considers the greater good of the ne'er-do-well, the
    greater story never told, the seven sins, the seven wonders,
    the seven dwarfs, ancient expectations, previous versions,
    the discontinued, the remaindered, the deleted, the disap-
    peared.
He, the dead man, being in fever and ardor, confirms that the frivolous
    is mixed up with the earnest, the make-believe with actuality,
    the old with the new, the living with the dead.
The dead man has littlemuch language for these precocious times.
What an era: the dead man poling for the bottom finds it fathomless.
For it was the nature of ethics to need language, however littlemuch.
The dead man has all the languages, the scripts, those based on sound,
    those based on picture, those based on interval, those soaked
    in adrenaline, those dry as English toast.
The dead man knows how hard it can be to speak with a mouthful of
    grit.
The dead man doesn't spit straight up.

2. More About the Dead Man and Little Much

It's little enough to be voiceless in a clamor.
The dead man shapes the din and the uproar, he puts potholes along the information superhighway, he blocks the ramps, he disconnects, he is off-line, he interferes.
The dead man knows the roads and the music, the wires and the keys, are there only to make the rats run faster.
The dead man tries on one hat at a time, he is persistence of vision incarnate, he is knowing of the binary two-step, he is formidably with-it, he is hip but he knows better.
The promises of knowledge, this genetic free-for-all, these complete records, this Big Brother that has your number, this non-stop news, this access, this roundly thumped privacy – the dead man witnesses each incursion into the far reaches of ignorance.
He thinks at this rate the gauges will break and the computers crash.
He sees the sundials wobbling nervously over what time it is.
He sees the stars leaning.
To the dead man, nothing more is something else, a concept beyond population and resources, an idea whose time is past.
He has littlemuch lingo, littlemuch answers, littlemuch solar longevity.
Whereby the dead man rocks the planet to sleep, the song still on his lips, his covenant unbroken.

MARJORIE BUETTNER

JULY 4th

Like a flower that knows
it will return to seed,
I have in me the presence
of a past which pigments the future.
Even when my husband,
after churning me into
a white-buttered heat,
dissolves into sleep, I
lie awake and feel each seed
from me fall back into a form
of forgetfulness or formlessness
or remorse I cannot tell.
Even after the thundering storm
which shakes the house as if it were
a liquid thing, I wait
and watch the boomerang of thoughts
(and time) fly back to encircle and
enclose until this concentric flight
creates in me a clean heart oh God.

THE HARMONICS OF SPRING

Morningtide in early spring,
rain shadows snow.
The air vibrates,
a pure ring,
with a cardinal's song,
cleaving, as well,
that silence in me
until we are as fine-tuned
as a single sound wave,
moving worlds, shattering moons,
light years away.

3 AM

Driving home at 3 a.m.
from a work that gnaws at my sleep
leaving me yellow and soft like a half-eaten apple,
I see at the stop the white exhaust in the rearview mirror
float up from the back then forward, preceding me.
It is shaped like a fading ghost,
captured in a flight it does not understand.
For a while,
I follow the eyes and
the beckoning finger
until it becomes a memory of
something else, of someone else.
I turn the wheel over and let the car
drive me home;
the scent of cloves still in the air.

JOHN DANIEL

CHINESE KIDNEYS

The Chinese use criminals' kidneys
for transplants.
Rich Americans pay $40,000
for fresh kidneys
The kidney donors are marched into a stadium
wearing yellow jackets like road workers
young unemployed men roaming China
guilty of theft or drug-dealing
they kneel down
hands behind their backs
the cord tied round the throat
so they don't make last-minute speeches
against the state
a bayonet is pushed into the back
so the body stiffens
then they are shot in the head.
A plain van drives up
and the kidneys are taken out immediately
They are fresher than American kidneys
a doctor says proudly
the wrong-doers are repaying their debts
to the state
which is building a new wing
to the hospital with the profits
white-tiled, luxury
unheard of in China
with en-suite bathrooms
for the visiting patients
just like America

I imagine the video reversing
the young men kneeling upright
the bayonet being pulled out
the backward march to the stadium
for the speeches and harangues
the young men returning the stolen goods
and then going in search of their kidneys
finding the customer sitting in a bar
paying the $40,000 back
the American saying, OK bud, it's yours
and picking up the dinner knife he carves out the kidney
and hands it back, soft and round as an egg
and falls forward over the table
as though he had been the one executed

SUCCESS

It was the 2nd Rayners Lane Cub Pack.
I was an Otter.
They were in sets like stamps
the red set
the blue set
the yellow set
shining like jewels in the dust
outside the Cub hut.
I wanted them all.
I set about gardening, first-aiding
and dusting under the bed.
My mother signed a certificate
swearing I had dusted under the bed.
I grew lettuces, applied tourniquets
and swam with my clothes on.
My father signed a certificate
swearing I had swum with my clothes on.
At last I had all of them.
Akela gave a speech in the pack
as we stood in a ring in the dust.
There Are More Important Things In Life
than Badges, he said.
Badges Were Not That Important.
I left the Otters and joined the Jackals.
I walked past the Club hut
and hid in the bike shed
where rubies shone in the dark
like mudguard reflectors
and an inner tube slid along in the dust,
hissing Success, Success, Success.

DON JOHN LEARNS TO KNIT

The Teddy Bear slayers have a lot to answer for.
— George Macbeth

Cubby was Don John's teddy bear
with silver-blue fur

Don John knitted him a silver-blue scarf
in over through off

French knitting, four nails in a cotton reel
a knitting of love

he took Cubby to bed with him
he was warm and friendly

in the ice-floe sheets
a silver-blue hotwater bottle

*

Bob was alive
a field spaniel

liver-and-white
thumping his tail on the mat

carrying four kids on his back
an open-jawed waddler

pink gums, tongue, brown eyes
with a white parting

Don John sat on the mat
lifted one of his curly pink-lined knitted ears

and told him everything

*

Cubby disappeared

the bed a desolate polar waste
no footprints on the pillow, nothing

Bob was put to sleep
Don John slept alone

in the arctic sheets
no more bears dogs

warmth mat hugs tongue
fur you could dig into

knitting
nothing

RUTH STONE

HUMMINGBIRDS

Driving the perfect fuel, its thermonuclear wings,
into the hot layer of the sugar's chromosphere,
hummingbirds in Egypt
might have visited the tombs of the Pharaohs
when they were fresh in their oils and perfumes.
The pyramids fitted,
stone slab against slab,
with little breathers, narrow slits of light,
where a few esters, a sweet resinous wind,
might have risen soft as a parachute.
Robbers breached the false doors,
the trick halls often booby traps,
embalming them in the powder of crushed rock.
These, too, they might have visited.
The miniature dagger hangs in the air
entering the wild furnace of the flower's heart.

A PAIR

The black and white cat
means to get off
the screened-in porch.
Castrated but suave,
he lives with this older woman
whose husband, dead thirty years,
secretly puts his cheek to hers
in a dime store photograph.
The children no longer visit.
The cat holds all the threads
of her detonated psyche.
He is the master key without
a lock. She picks him up.
The porch screen has been mended.
He thinks there are the old openings.
Birds, insects leap
out of the flecked light.
Inside the screen, her hands
stroke his electric body.

DON'T MISS IT

If you're looking for a heron on one leg,
or a white egret in this water-logged parcel,
you may be blind to boarded-up gas pumps,
flashes of sleazy mock-up towns;
though finally, a rusted roof,
gaping shed or wizened trailer
may appear like strange fowl
as you snake on past dry bayous
where the old jalopies flake to crust,
splintering their jumping joy-juice;
battered bodies, the good old boys left behind.

A GOOD QUESTION

Look at these disparate shapes.
The air is displaced
by the bulk of the table.
The table is borrowed.
For that matter, the chair is plastic.
Altogether, the square room
is concealed from the snow.
The snow falls for nine hours.
Occasionally on the sly
I raise up the window.
An implosion of temperatures
condenses steam to water.
How can I live like this?

THE APEX

If there could be another time like that,
when all your ancestors and all of mine
conspired to bring us together. Back there
on the savanna in the days when we touched
the earth with our palms. Whose deep set eyes
and heavy arms shoved all those others aside?

And yet, my love, you were so delicate; the flicker
of an almost infinite lightning, an infinitely small
leaping quanta, like the tracery of the universe,
that was yourself, the strangeness of the animal.

TIMOTHY HODOR

ON THE FERRY TO AN ISLAND OF EXILE

We leave Piombino.
The waves splash silence.

The dusk whispers over Elba.
We approach Portoferraio.

A lighthouse works
Like a pair of compasses

Pivoting on the sea.
Waves of black arcs drown.

THE LAST WORD

There's a shadow of speech we do not hear:
It is mute and has our contours.
It's a hollow voice that one day
Comes inside us and fills our mouth with air,
Then forces our tongue behind our teeth,
And makes us say – death.

LEE LARCOMB

FIVE STAIRSTEPS TO THE ANT FARM

On the first step, you lose your
balance
and pretend to fall. your skin becomes
dark green and the air around you
smells like shit. Hands from the walls
reach out to you. & a voice like carnival joes
starts to say a word that you once had
to look up in the dictionary.

*

The ants hide their real faces
in dirt roads
the flavor of 100-year-old wagon wheels.
It is a sight which you will never forget.

*

participate.
participate.
participate.

*

On this step, a swiss cuckoo clock
unwinds itself in slow motion.
The wooden bird knows your name by heart
& is often called "feather brain".

*

On the final step, there is a birthday party.
with devils food cake. & melty ice cream.
& 20 bold candles.
The honored guest is Mr. Faust, cleansing
each one of the candles
                                        as though they were
his fingers.

HOW GLOOM CITY GOT ITS NAME

for lack of anything
better to do.
in the blue danube
with 3.2 beer and dean.
we had noticed how clouds manipulated
our lives
with the regularity
of the b&o brakeman's gold watch.
in recent months
we had even taken up painting.
poetry. & mexican food as an antidote.
we named it as a convict
might call a shadow of the gallows.

lee larcomb

DREAM SEQUENCE

You are there
as always.
I am moving

into an old
white house.
You are there

on the top floor
in a brass bed.
The walls are black.

There is a glow
behind you.
Your skin is outlined,

white.
I speak out
fragments;

phrases
of Russian.
You cannot hear.

I am crying.
My tears become
fog.

You smile
through the fog.
And I begin to move.

Then I am blind.
The pillow throbs
like your heart.
And I can distinctly remember
the words for *five* and *apples*.

28.VI.69

<u>LESLIE ADRIENNE MILLER</u>

THE HISTORY OF RHETORIC

> *Writing, Phaedrus, has this strange quality, and it is like painting; for the creatures of painting stand like living beings, but if one asks them a question, they preserve a solemn silence.*
>
> – *Socrates to Phaedrus in the* Phaedrus

> *...the self identity of the signified conceals itself unceasingly and is always on the move.*
>
> – *Derrida*, Of Grammatology

Last night I dreamed Plato, Socrates
and Phaedrus were a conflation
of animated lines, one ancient man,
white bearded, robed, oddly barefoot.
It was imperative that I tell them
apart, yet I could not. When I woke
the man beside me asked me to speak
about love. And I had only those
three speeches, two against love, one for.
Poor Phaedrus, so sure of his goodness,
but fascinated with the eloquence
of the heretical. Socrates wins
but only because Plato arranges it.
Socrates is too glib and really lusts
after whatever it is Phaedrus carries
beneath his cloak. My lover too wants
whatever is beneath my silence,
a speech he thinks I hide.
But I am afraid to speak and always
have been; truth, it seems, escapes too easily
because the bars on the cage were spaced

for larger prey. The sound of my voice
has always surprised me, so tiny, tentative,
not the voice I thought would be there,
nor the one I trusted to answer well.

Instead I regard an orange cat who sits
in a page of sunlight. His business is hush,
his genes tell him: *deadly stillness*,
and only his eyes move toward the bird
he must have. But the bird is caught
in my throat while my lover puts on a blue sock,
blue exactly the same as his shirt.
If I were to speak I would say:
How consoling that blue is.
He stops with the second sock, looks at it hard,
waiting. *Why don't you speak to him*?
my mother asked over and over
when we passed a boy she knew I knew.
I never answered. I was thinking
of something dropped in the street,
something we passed too quickly
for me to say what it was.

The silence between a question and its answer
is that page of sunlight, so intense
you cannot see its source. I look into it
for a long time and am astonished
at how much has been turned
like told dreams into narrow certainty.
Plato was not just Plato in the dream,
but a grid of ideas I could see moving across
each other. Waking, it is only Plato and
the Socrates he made, whose seduction
of truth is all the usual torment and wise-crack.
As a child I made the silence I wanted
out of the chalk dust, out of the murky light.

I made the tall man speaking math
a hum, and then a whisper, then nothing.
There is no trouble in silence. The trees
outside looking down at their waists,
the vines holding fast to the fence,
shadows inching away.

Now I give my silence to love's paralysis.
The bedclothes in a mute knot. Those blue
socks in which there is no grief.
No grief in the porcelain roses on the lamp,
in the green coffee cup I love above
all others in the cupboard, in the fan blades
circling so perfectly above us. They have
no plot. As long as I look at them and say nothing
there is no action, only the hush of motion
in this world, in which it is impossible
that I could ever disappoint anyone.

JONATHAN SISSON

QUABIC

On Old Highway 61
along the shore northeast of Duluth
Fats Domino takes a break in “So Long,”

and a soprano sax goes wild:
Quabic, quabic, quabic, quabic, quabic…
and has another forty quabics to go

when from behind an oncoming car
someone catapults into the air,
and a rear-ending motorcycle floats up,

the rider still rising,
christopher-reeving aloft
like O.J. Simpson in *The Naked Gun.*

Yes, I took a hundred photos.
Here you can see her helmet.
Her trajectory is quite easy to chart.

The wind’s not a factor.
She’s veering left, arcing toward my lane
to alight on my front bumper some half second from now.

But there are many nows,
and the road has a broad shoulder,
and I’m not too drowsy from lunch.

When I stop and run back,
she's prone, motionless, in my lane.
In a while she says her knee is all.

O my guardian angel,
she's alive because you whispered,
"Take a light lunch, and skip dessert for once."

SONG OF THE THICKET

Rhapsody on a Theme of Sam Peabody

Wild Lake Superior roses and raspberries,
lonesome lost loons in their fog-ridden ghostliness,
sea gulls decrying perfidious outrages,

cool upland forests of balsam-ripe undergrowth
near meadows thronged by dog fennel and buttercup,
thick bird's-foot trefoil and hawkweed and columbine,

red-clay back roads for the squirrels and garter snakes,
wolf-scat lumps cluttered with cloudbursts of sootywings,
old farmsteads fallen to white-throated sparrow flocks.

These North Shore property claims are worth singing for,
though Jonvick Creek is a treacherous paradise.
Sweet, sweet, oh, sweet are the dangers of nest building.

MALLARDS

Startled, a mallard drake
and his two wives
and nine May ducklings
break from the pond sedge,
the ducklings fast regrouping
as they swim
in four and five,
close constellated fears,
knowing their mothers
by what scent or quack,
as I could sense my son,
some other boy
related distantly
to this weird ghost
in his white toga
for the Latin club.
Somewhere between,
at some mysterious age,
that brief inhuman love
must have dissolved,
maybe in the cold harbor
of Duluth
in the fall thunderstorm
when the grain ships
heeled over like beached whales,
and mallard ducklings
followed their mothers
into the black waves.

CANDLELIGHT VIGIL

October 1986

On a cold and moonless October night
on the broad steps of the Minnesota state capitol,
in jeans and corduroys, leather jackets and mauve parkas,
Greek caps, berets, hoods, headbands, hair blowing,
familiar eyes shining, they are holding votive candles
flickering in clouded plastic drinking cups,
in honor of four army veterans fasting
a month now on the steps of the nation's capitol
to protest the new war against Nicaragua.

The media shame themselves in silence of the fast
and of the racketeers ravaging our economy again.
Banks of huge floodlights bathe the capitol
of gray-streaked marble in arches and angels,
festoons and wreaths, four champing golden chariot steeds,
figures of Osiris and Isis and sacrificed farmers.
The marble glares dead white against the black sky,
a facade fake as a plywood Hollywood set.
Dark pigeons lurk in rows in the cavern shadow.

A flock of bright birds bursts round the lit cupola,
flaring out shimmering like the capitol's aura,
startled cherubim escaped from a domed ceiling,
starlight shaken from the flag of broken promises,
patriotic fireworks of the shattered spirit
veering together with the sweep of guttering candles,
phantom migrant rock doves glittering and gathering
for a fall flight to the Central American forests,
the furies and only phoenix of the embattled heart.

THE PELICANS AT SHAKOPEE

White pelicans riding the thermal
above a country fair,
a sixteenth-century English village,
roil in the torrid air
and turn a hundred with a flockwide flash
like half-burnt flakes of ash.

From the marsh lakes of Manitoba,
banking with a slow roll
and soaring on their nine-foot wingspread,
they spiral in a scroll
of cryptic characters in black and white
about their strenuous flight.

The fairgoer reads a cold September,
a sudden early frost.
His fathers dust-bowled half the topsoil
that Indian chiefs had lost,
and now he plays a subject of Queen Bess,
when this was wilderness.

He joins the royal costume party:
late Renaissance and crass,
drunk lords and ladies sway around him
like the tall prairie grass.
Elizabethan pelicans would bleed
to feed their nestlings' greed.

As falcon, barn owl, golden eagle
cruise in a fairground show,
the pelicans think home for winter,
the Gulf of Mexico,
and meantime dance their fishing circle high
together in the sky.

THE DOOR OF THE DEAD

Careening through the strait called Porte des Morts
takes much more luck than knowledge to prevail
against the winds and currents at Death's Door.

Five hundred Winnebago braves at war
were swept aside and drowned on the coup trail
careening through the strait called Porte des Morts.

A winter storm in 1864
iced Robert Noble round, to hack and flail
against the winds and currents at Death's Door

and thrash his way into the county lore.
His feet and fingers gone, he told the tale
careening through the strait called Porte des Morts.

The Simonsons, each frozen to his oar,
were driven by a February gale
against the winds and currents at Death's Door

and looked alert with their heads turned toward shore
that spring when someone saw their ice floe sail
careening through the strait called Porte des Morts
against the winds and currents at Death's Door.

CALVIN FORBES

BONGO DANCING

this fella who says rhythm
it's not so important
he don't know polka from mambo

take physics it has to be exact
and philosophy too
no hip cat can do that

even if he study xyz
what's so rare about rhythm
can you breathe it eat it make love to it

then I figure out the problem
how he gonna calypso bop
do the wild thing when his science

still counting sheep
he don't know titty from can can
he don't know how to dance

whole dance with just the eyes
and he calling rhythm easy
like he the Pope

MOMMA'S BOY BLUES

I told my inlaws I told my outlaws
see how one hand treat the other

sometimes the people closest to you
turn out to be so far away

you ever seen a grown woman cry
her face lonely as one eye

I told my inlaws I told my outlaws
something's got to give

maybe it's time I gave up the ghost
you ever seen a grown woman cry

like she an angel calling you home
she rocks she rocks

I told my inlaws I told my outlaws
you ever make your woman cry

like your daddy did your momma
nobody cry pretty not even a baby

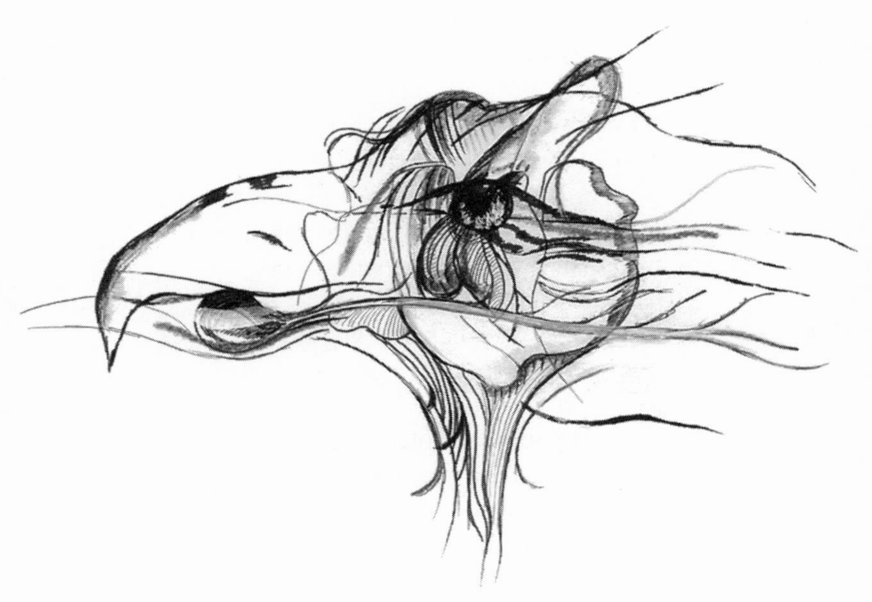

JULIA BUDENZ

TIMES WITH THE TEASE IN

1.

If you would answer we might well converse.
You spoke, and I replied, and that was all.
I, ever rusty, listened in the fall
To words that March had labored to disburse

Through reams of August into autumn's purse
Which twinkled with the golden coins that call
Their estimates across the urban sprawl
And dwindling fields through which the gilded hearse

Travels the amber track of time. And now
Will winter whiten into that great lie
Burying purple soundlets out of view

(I should say, out of hearing), or, somehow,
Will utterance that must be mine or I
Surge with the snowdrops into yours and you?

Note on Poem: "Times with the Tease In" and "Bounds That Let Breeze In" are the last two of the five parts of the sequence "To Bruce Bennett, Richard Rorty, Quintus Horatius Flaccus, et al.," which occurs in a section that follows "Conversations with the Italian" and precedes "Vision" in Book Three, "Rome," of the poem in five books, "The Gardens of Flora Baum." - *JB*

2.

But to be worthy of the conversation
Will one have learned the language, played the game,
Stridden along the stage, embraced acclaim,
Wresting the least satanic connotation,

Wrestling the most angelic concentration,
From pit or bleachers, infamy or fame,
Bull's ear, wild curved boar's tail, a sheep's most tame
Curl, or those curling anthems from the nation

Of birds that settle or from birds that pass
As though a momentary note could say
Enough for ecstasies of sun or sorrow?

I hear fine droplets light upon the grass.
Must prized pearls, must praised daisies, win today
The accolade of welcoming tomorrow?

3.

Vendere: scendere;
Vivere: scrivere;

O

To love: to live;
To do: to die;
To save: to sieve;
To see: to say: to sigh:

L'infinito: the infinitive.

4.

To hear or to have heard or else to hope
That from the glitter-gleam of silver speech
Nutlet will find itself gigantic beech
Or, to effect a turning in the trope,

Silvery strands will twist themselves to rope
Both long enough and strong enough to reach
And grip the branch from which each thread and each
Connection linking threads sustains the scope

Inherent in the activated swing
Becomes the subject. Will the finite verb
Convey, although beloved elms were felled

For failing at the testing of the spring,
If others spread above campaign and curb,
The messages which lengths of summer held?

5.

Why do I say what only seems to jar
Those who might want to hear what I might say
If I could sink my silver into gray
Or raise up out of mud a golden bar?

Why does the tree rise proudly as a czar
And reach across the overshadowed way
If those who pass compel the tree to pay
For greenest sovereignty with blackest scar?

Why does the bird lift to the distant star
Cantatas which the sleepy neighbors pray
Will terminate before impatient day
Tethers bronze horses to the golden car?

Why do I love what only seems to bore
Those who might want to glean what I adore?

6.

Listen, Letitia, lover of that breath
That sweeps upon you silently from skies
That offer you, before the body dies,
Balms that desiderate the body's death.

Visions, Letitia, greet you on the path
That climbs to summits where the mortal eyes
Widen like cornets wreathed to solemnize
Instants of sempiternal aftermath.

Morsels of matter let the vision live.
Bits of the earthy dark arise to feed
The spirit's lightest breathings. O, consent

To bend and take the particles that give
Strengths that the highest chiming wingbeats need.
The body is the spirit's instrument.

7.

I said that I would do it. Did I state
I would have done it? Did I then await
A future or a past

Or something that would last
Longer: the future in the past, the late
Lingering tempo, tense with time's strange date?

8.

I beat my breast, I, hypocrite auteur.
I listened, yet I listened just enough
To scrape from erudition's pile the fluff.
O speak more loudly through the veils, ma soeur.

Then is the mea culpa de rigueur
Or may I plead the denseness of the stuff
That intervenes, tied scarf or handled muff,
Between the hearer and the cri de coeur?

If I had understood a little more
Would I have curved my fist around the throttle
Of my response and not crouched here alone

Fitting my phrases neatly to the drawer,
Crushing my clauses deeply down the bottle,
Leaving my sentence on the telephone?

9.

You said this, you said this, and you said this,
And you said this and that, and you and you
Said that. And there were others, more or few,
Who said some other thing, and did I miss

The ones whose contradictions raised a hiss
Throughout the throng? Did someone give a view?
Did one or many tell us what was true?
Did any doom us down the deaf abyss?

We gathered at the banquet on the hill.
We stretched our hands to bread and reached for wine.
We gathered there for better or for worse.

We banqueted till all had had their fill.
We talked. We talked unendingly. Come, dine.
Come and converse with us. Come and converse.

BOUNDS THAT LET BREEZE IN

1.

The sonnet sent by electronic mail
Offers itself to its recipient
Perhaps as purely an impediment
To conversation on the sober scale

That holds the future and that must prevail
Over the weights and measures prevalent
In centuries profoundly different,
When convents kept their nuns within the pale.

When castles kept their queens and their queens' daughters
Within the battlements securely zipped,
Would I have held a feather in my hand

For fingered flights across a manuscript
Or scribbled with a pebble on the sand
Or rippled rhythms into ebbing waters?

2.

If from her head they snatched the sacred veil
And if they pulled the pure ring from her hand
Shall we confess that we misunderstand
Their times? Shall we acknowledge that we fail

To read the heart beating beneath the mail,
Compute the mind beneath the miter, and
Inscribe within our righteous reprimand
Our times in paragon? The jealous jail

That holds our sisters holds the holders of
Its key. Did fathers, uncles, brothers bind
Piccarda panting for the chosen part,

Costanza constant to the holiest love,
Her ring the radiant halo of her mind,
Her veil the somber guardian of her heart?

3.

It was an error, for my pious hand
Could not have torn that sweetness from the tree.
I walked with one who robbed that sweet for me.
I held the lilac which that loveliest land

Lifted to us. I held that we were banned
From violation. He maintained that he
Who walked among the blossoms must be free
To take and keep. I held the smoking brand.

The fragrant exhalation which it gave,
No, every scent which echoed in that air
From every branch which flourished into fume,

Was sigh, was sign, was speaking. Could you bear
To lacerate your mother? Does the bloom
Droop? Will the lilac drop into a grave?

4a.

If I should tell you you could not believe.
The forest bristled and the forest groaned.
The black leaves whistled and the white twigs moaned.
If you should snap a branch you could retrieve

A truth. The meaning, if I could conceive
A merest meaning, merely was postponed
As my mind slowly, slowly, slowly owned
What my hand, hesitating, could achieve.

I plucked a twiglet from the trunk. A gruel
Dripped forth its syllables. You could not gain
A knowledge of its words just from my verse.

Through wounds alone could man turned plant converse.
Could the guide master poet then be cruel?
Or did he know that speech is worth the pain?

4b.

She grabbed it with her hand or with her foot.
But if her arms were wings the monstrous claw
Must have evolved on legs to let her put
Her mug into the mass that stuffed her maw.

The ravenous voracity that craves
The ravenous voracity that gluts
The ravenous voracity that raves
Is gluttony that satiates the guts

Aging insatiable. The greed that grasps
At gold is ancient, famed. The holy hunger
That like the newest nestling gapes and gasps
To know is older and forever younger.

Will she hear, see, talk, master alphabets?
Oh, will the sun come out before it sets?

4c.

My feet now stand at last upon the top.
My hands, that helped me often at the start
When, timely quadruped, I bore the smart
Of stubborn steep upon my forepaws, stop.

Only my eyes move now. My hands may drop
Until that aftertime when my hand's art
Will strive to scrive on parchment what my heart
Records here from my eyes. No further prop

Is necessary to sustain the sight
Or the sight's monuments. The purple finch
Dawns on the bough. The budding noontide roses

Warm gold and rose and gold. Fresh violet light
Rings lilac, lavender, last hyacinth.
The vision opens, and the codex closes.

5a.

The pacifist who falls in love with Rome
Is tortured by a passion unbenign
And born beneath the Castors' double sign.
Both Mars and Venus splashed with Tiber's foam

The rosy youth who bloomed in royal dome:
Pallas descending from the Palatine,
Pallas advancing through the battle line,
Pallid Pallas carried as ashes home.

Is there no truce? Is one to be content
To wage or to endure eternal war
Or suffer or enjoy a Roman peace?

If Janus has two faces, one is bent
Upon the world. The other cannot cease
To glimpse the universe of metaphor.

5b.

The persons may be second, third, or first.
The terms may be divergent or the same.
Aeneas may not be the proper name.
I am the Dante whom Firenze nursed.

I am the Dante whom Firenze cursed.
I am the man who went to hell and came
Back from the brightness of celestial flame
Unblinded. Pity once kept my lips pursed.

Connections can be purest persiflage.
The thinker as the scribbler may be weak.
The dreamer and the poet are distinct.

The author and the agent are not linked.
What self indwells the pious personage
Who only speaks to say he cannot speak?

5c.

Will it be Rome if at the swampside shrine
I find the goddess or the goddesses
Celebrated on that narrow line
Where the sun stops? The celebration is

The debt of death, the credit of a choice
Of a great conversation, a conversion
That from the bandaged mouth returns a voice
That from the narrow passage flaunts emersion,

The moral of a more that follows less,
The lessons of December twenty-first,
Concentration and expansiveness,
The dark constriction and the bright outburst,

Angerona and Volupia,
Pain of today and pleasure of, ah . . ., ah . . .

5d.

The first city was not the final one.
We built its walls. Its name endures today
As Aenus from my own. We did not stay.
The bleeding bush exhorted us to run.

Copernicus will send us to the sun.
The center must await the émigré.
We launch, and lands and cities move away.
So might the vision slip from the kneeling nun.

The virgin's veil became the scholar's hood.
The vow yielded the hope that holds in view
The doubtful and the unequivocal.

Poverty is selection of the good,
Obedience submission to the true,
Chastity rapture by the beautiful.

5e.

The mother of my home god has her home
Here. Will examined witnesses prove wrong?
And can her habitation rhyme with Rome,
Where I have never walked? The road is long.

The road has been so long. The twenty-third
Sun of the year's last moon is here, and now.
And now is here. Here is forever heard
Calling afar from near the distant plow

That liberates the city from the marsh
And promises the building of the wall
Which separates the city from the harsh
Regime of Mars. Mother, will here still call?

When the priest calls the Calends from the hill
Will I be there to hear or be here still?

5f.

What is that crash? The narrow room is thick
With forest. From the floorboards to the ceiling
Brusque spines, shoots, shrubs, trunks, trees have sprung,
  concealing
Wall, window, bookshelf, table, chair. Each stick

Barricades each. Solidity. A flick,
A flicker, is unthinkable. Revealing
The limitations of all thought and feeling,
The supervention, in an augenblick,

Of that vast mind-ear-earth-shattering crash
Suffers supervention. What is that crack?
What is that wild and horrend boarlike strage?

What is that plant ensanguined from the gash?
Who is that person under that attack
Wracking his personhood? I turn the page.

5g.

If Pallas died to give the eagle sway
Can we deny that Dante comprehends
How the long story of Aeneas ends?
For Rome was not constructed in a day.

On the great battlefield the young man lay
Slain by the enemy who made amends
By being slain. Destruction simply tends
Towards its own deconstruction. Far away

Force its fierce condestruction. Reap at home
After the final Twelve the sacred spelt
Sown in Book Ten and watered in Eleven.

If Pallas died to sanction holy Rome
Can we deny that Dante knew and felt
The lit crit and the politics of Heaven?

6a.

Big-bellied, starving Harpies made the rents
With their clawed, clawing feet that let the breeze
Of utterance release disharmonies
For which the lacerations were the vents.

Their necks were human, and their long laments
Were strange but human in the stranger trees.
The trees were human, and their miseries
Wintered civilization's discontents.

There was no path around each brambly patch.
There was no way for any wayfarer.
I recognized the spined amphiboly.

Was I the hunter? I the easy catch?
Was I the pilgrim, stranger, foreigner?
Was I the bird? Was I the talking tree?

6b.

The Latin lamentations of the leaves
Had grown from human throat, and they were mine.
The English expletives around the eaves
Were screamed by harpies of another line.

The Latin lamentations were the howl
Of one who loved the umbra of the elm
But whose eruptions ever were found foul,
Corruptions of the vegetable realm.

The harpy, starving starling, winged debris,
Hooked hands and clawed with feet upon faint fame,
Proprietor or tenant of the tree
Named elm of daydream. Why contest the name?

Landlady Malaprop, despising starlings,
Evicted them but always called them darlings.

6c.

Will there be enemies? Must there be war?
Is it at my own feet that Turnus lies
Turning that suppliant hand, those suppliant eyes,
While these eyes roll and this hand sticks before

Swordbelt and sword determine either-or?
The bad but breathing barrier now dies,
The grand and good and godly goal will rise.
Does the famed savior face the savage boar

In bannered combat, final, fine, and thorough?
And does the fated founder grasp and solve
The problem of the blessing and the curse?

The plow turns at the furling of the furrow.
The roll must roll, the volume must revolve.
The end is not the ending of the verse.

7.

Shall I be silent? Shall I explicate?
Does terror render loud or render mute
The prophetess attentive to the root
From which deterrent phrases sanguinate

And to the boughs that bleed the words of fate?
Blood was the price here of a priceless loot.
Blood is of blood this solitary fruit.
You will devour your table with your plate.

Gathering branches for the sacrifice,
I heard the proclamation of despair.
The term, term of my feet, Rome stayed in scope.

In Rome the terrifying tableware
Could be the crunchy, thick, delicious slice
Of bread that bases banqueting on hope.

8.

Therefore look well, for that way you will see
Things that would make you doubt my conversation,
Said bard to bard. The visive revelation
Kept coming on the feet of poetry

That walks and talks with such as you and me,
Enticing eyes, requiring auscultation,
Taking my hand, propelling your oration,
Rendering Polydore and Peter free

To speak of plantedness. The insite force
Of rest and movement is rush and repose
Of sight and converse. Drink the deeper fount.

Not only whirlpools but that gleaming course,
Not only prickles but this purpled rose,
Not only headlines but a verse may count.

9.

I am ensnared. My words cannot be bought,
But I am helpless. You compel reply.
One whom their francs and florins could not buy
Your utterance alone has called and caught.

The net of text entwined, entwining, ought
To bind. It binds the feet. It frees the cry.
It forces song. It frees the song. And I,
Unpaid and uninvited and unsought,

Tin drummer, brazen trumpeter, I dare,
O ancient mellow ones, O great though gray,
O grand and solid silver, sterling, true,

O great and golden, burnished, burning, fair
Darlings, strong, eminent - what shall I say? -
If I can talk at all to talk to you.

JOE PADDOCK

DARK BOX

An old dark
wooden box
continues in my dream, disturbed
by old Louie's gruff calling
to his dogs on the pre-dawn
sidewalk outside,
pulling me up from center,
here at the center
of this town surrounded
by burial mounds, stone cairns
of bones heaped over, a people
whose living bones leaped here
long before even the Dakota.

The box, softly continuing
flower of mind, is connected somehow
to Fred Manfred, our storyteller
so recently dead, but connected
not just to Fred, not just
a tiny coffin or container of all
his stories, their energy compressed
as if a sun within, immense
with inner explosions. No,
the old dark
wooden box, continuing
as I sink again toward the center
of the moon, contains all
origins, the big bang expanding
at the speed of light to become

heaps of bones, the Dakota, us,
our stories, and arthritic old Louie.
stumping along at the tail end of the night
with his pair of labradors,
one dark and one light.
The dark one, Queenie, so old
and arthritic (even more so than Louie)
that she can't keep up, sometimes just sits
on a square of sidewalk, smiling
in sad apology and love
for her gruff-voiced master.

I see Queenie, in mind,
and old Fred, too, smiling,
as Louie's impatient calling
pulls me up and out from
the dark box of sleep
from which we all come.

GARY DECRAMER REMEMBERING FRED MANFRED

In the first feathering of light,
before the sun, Fred
would stand on the edge
of his bluff, overlooking
the world, his Siouxland
through rising mist.
His great trailing hands
would caress the tips of tall grasses
that reached to the root of things.

Somewhere near a meadowlark
would sing to him, the world, the wonder
of the rising sun.
Those two singers there,
and Fred would sniff,
would taste the wind,
breathing in the dawn's air
and song.

Calm, that peopled imagination
calm, and Fred, alive
as any eagle, gazing
out over his realm.

Breakfast
talk that contained
the power of the rising sun,
that swept like wind
over bending brome and bluestem,
the history of our people,
talk that crackled
like fire through stands
of ripened corn,

a continual harvest, and
listening, we knew
that the mind of this man
behind the dawn-blaze of his eyes
had *awakened*
to this morning, and
the blazing blue, the voice crackling
awakened *us*, too, and we
began our day believing
that some raw god truly was
in us, and we
could do anything.

Edna St. Vincent Millay

ON EDNA ST. VINCENT MILLAY

Millay has been dismissed and regarded as deeply out of date. The dismissal has partly to do with formal matters – her obsession with or capture by the romantic four-beat iambic line – and partly to do with gender matters. There appeared to be a certain passivity in Edna St. Vincent Millay that opened her to being carried away by four-beat lines or pirates. She didn't fight back until the middle of her life. She was constantly falling in love and then being abandoned, and her poems would speak out from that place of abandonment or "passive suffering," as Yeats called it. When women readers got tired of that receptive, passive role, they stopped reading Millay. I want to go on and look at her genuine power and tremendous genius with the image. In "Wine from These Grapes," she begins:

> Wine from these grapes I shall be treading surely
> Morning and noon and night until I die.
> Stained with these grapes I shall lie down to die.

There's something very fine here in using the stain from grape skins and all their old associations with Dionysus and Bacchus as an image for being incarnated into a body. She goes on:

> If you would speak with me on any matter,
> At any time, come where these grapes are grown;
> And you will find me treading them to must.
> Lean then above me sagely, lest I spatter
> Drops of the wine I tread from grapes and dust.

Except for the awkward rhyme of 'must' and 'dust,' the lines are really superb. She sees that the more abstract or puritanical types will have to be careful not to be spattered by her poem. She continues this way:

Stained with these grapes I shall lie down to die.
Three women come to wash me clean
Shall not erase this stain.
Nor leave me lying purely
Awaiting the black lover.

This is very surprising. The sudden appearance of this story about the three women alerts us to something new, and suddenly a black lover appears. We will find that the color black belongs not to race but to the world of Hades, who was, like his surroundings, black. Millay ends the poem:

Death, fumbling to uncover
My body in his bed,
Shall know
There has been one
Before him.

The sexual woman here playfully insists that others have been with her before the present lover. Death is not deeply humiliated, but a little, and he deserves it. These lines have the truthfulness of D. H. Lawrence and the formal elegance of H.D. and some of the bravery of Pound when he moved out of formal meters. So I think we need to honor her not only for her formal work, which is presently out of vogue, but for her superb imagery and truth-telling in her free verse.

ROBERT BLY

NILS PETERSON

MORNING IN MONTANA, JUNE, 1993

for William Stafford (1914-1993)

Someone's opened the cabin door
and stands a shadow between
the stove air and the mountain
cold. He runs his hands along

the doorposts, then up across
the lintel, seeming to measure,
seeming to feel for its shape
and size. It is Bill Stafford.

He vanishes, then reappears,
his hands again searching
to know this door. He senses
my open eyes, then really

disappears. Later I ask,
was it you? what were you doing?
He smiles at me and will not
admit and will not explain.

JAMES LONGSTAFF

END OF SEASONS

95. Iowa sun steam.
Belly of July.
Spinning rods lie in our johnboat's bow
Like exaggerated mimes of your legs.
Light as a heron's frame you ride,
Bank walker, hipbooted river wader, father.
Astern, I read the back of you.
Your hand, a knuckled web on a gunnel,
Held mine the day you pointed out
Pools my first hooked worm should plumb.
That withered arm taught me
The choreography of flyrods.
On your shoulders, now just planes of bone,
Your laced and buckled life vest hangs.
How loosely it enfolds you.
Here, let me! I would hold you up
In this – your river of 55 seasons –
And float you beyond the bend, there
Where your river runs into the earth.

james longstaff

CELEBRATION OF THE BI-COLORED CONVEYANCE

Know I'm in The City
By the green and yellow
Checker.
Hail the bump and rumble
Cab.
Slide on vinyl.
Slam the door.
"Clark and Belden.
Take the Drive."
Ride in the drum:
Run Michigan.
Bluff the limo.
Beat the light.
Click! . . .The Drake and
Bore the tunnel.
Funneled thunder.
Click! . . .The Drive.
Skin The Lake and
Exit Fullerton.
Lincoln Park . . .Click!
Curb on Clark.
Angled.
Pulsing.
Turns me out.
Jumps with a growl
To the hunt again.
Gone.
Signature of City –
Green and yellow Checker.
Street steel hooking
Chicago's ride.

GERARD MALANGA

RETURN TO PARIS AFTER TWO YEARS

Paul Blackburn, his line :

To create the situation / is love

and to avoid it, this is also
Love.

Fate being a double-edged sword
What if… what if
the situation be repeated again:
You're running, see ?
before the doors close at Galerie Donguy
You're running half out of breath

the Rue de la Roquette,
in the fading light, the chill air.
You are dodging the evening shoppers,

swinging out toward the curb edge,
standing in the street simply.
An apple, orange, deux cahiers.
You have your Nikon wrapped in plastic
to keep from getting wet,
but then you arrive.
The lights are out (next time maybe.)
Everyone has since left,
so the photos we have of
each other are not of
each other,
as if the past were anything else but

what it is. Luck is
always for tomorrow. Luck is
starcrossed. Luck is
something forever gone and again renewed.
So-called "chapter" you once said,
to begin anew,
to grow from that – and
repeated often enough
even the word looks empty, despite the hope,
despite the smell of hot flesh.
It is not Spring in Amsterdam.
It is the Month of the Photo in Paris.
It is again 1992.
It is windless here.
No, it does not rain.
I called out to her,

feel the warmth
and as she turned,
I suddenly woke.
15:xii:94 Paris

VASE WITH FLOWERS

Fate has it the world didn't exist
as when you meet someone – the
occurrence of that period
                                        in some such way
as this
termed "meaningful coincidence,"
recognized as such
                                the choice
to deny or fulfill   the fear also

Leaves all gone now. Sky's crisp and clear.
Skin bronzed in the shaded light.

This is the world of the imagination.
This is a photo of Virginia
last year in Amsterdam.

1:1:94 Great Barrington, MA

DE KOONING'S *EXCAVATION*

To be in the stroke,
to be a "slipping glimpser,"
to slip the stroke while glimpsing paralysis
          in its metamorphics,
        the cobblestone over tectiforms,
      Huitzilopochtli under Jesus smears

Excavation of the parking lot next door,
fresh worm-severed dirt walls,
   hole,   oldest habitation,
intercourse of basement-to-be-built
                              with
                    building-to-be-built,
two heads locked jaws within jaws

          Painting is the coming of an infant,
annunciation at the corner of Carmine Street,
                there is a way to foal
in dismemberment,   to strike coal
      on sound pounce

   Tectiform   Techtiform   tent or sail or
forearm vertical, beginning or ending with a fist?
Add another forearm,   arm-wrestling with self
       is prayer,   let's shake on sorrow,
    no way to begin again? Begin at the end,
                                          consider Gauguin:

Europe diseased, naturalism finished, trees grew blue,
  lizards braided Tahitian Eve,
Gauguin exposed an eco-ethnopoetic morass that still
  shudders,   he implied: to envision
is to recast Genesis,   he wrapped his legs in rags
  to conceal the syphilis

What is it to run
the end backwards? Slinky Nude
  step by step ascending,
attic,
the last to be built contains the oldest

Totem pole: at the top center of *Excavation*
a bird head beak
dings the roof of the Font-de-Gaume-like tectiform.
Its base, a cocktail tray, is held up by an upraised hand's
splayed fingers & thumb,   which splay is also
  the mouth of a head from whose severed neck
flame fills the space between a seated suited man &
his mostly-effaced double,   he's seated on a filled
  bra suspended over the second tectiform
(at the totem's base), to the left of which
a guffawing man's head is being munched into,
to the right of which spread upraised legs diamond down –

It took me a quarter hour to see this totem
a second now to watch lipstick jabs and semen-yellow linoleum
scuffed with cartoon heads & cleavers engulf the totem

The Maya Underworld argues the subconscious is the realm of
unending beheading,   to which de Kooning appends
jaw-locked heads sprouting shark snouts or crown-like keds
                                        – Soutine draws near,
he's just crawled out of his Montparnasse plot,
shaken the bedbugs from his head,   a headlock secures him

The bare-recognizable is jigsawed to voids
                              which become forms
discharging former barely-recognizables
Is there a safe house here? No –
is there a safe house for No? Yes –
Ophelia crawling the Milky Way is
Blondie scrubbing the Bumstead kitchen floor is
a child on a living room floor studying the Sunday comics
  through layers of wispy feeling between the legs
  of his laughing parents is
Ophelia crawling Dagwood,   her ear is his open mouth
    Midden compressed into a painting,
the skull from Level H forced to interact with
    the femur from Level Y,
de Kooning's dream mind pressed,
  like a parental insect-filled night.
between two glass plates,   larvatory of lares & lemurs,
Gorgon carotid dousing Pegasus,
inspiration & its analogues

Excavation is a jigsaw solved before our eyes,
we know it is a puzzle
because of the tourbillion of its parts

Condrum of the abstract,
more concrete than real,
it invites us to set the primal scene on fire

Multiple thimble lock of
the member-flung wreckage, *Medusa*
on which the slithering & appealing
are snakes, held against bandsaws

Red knife nipple agrow in breast.

23 July 1995

JANE SPIRO

REVOLUTION IN KASHMIR

Sandalwood pared
from boatpeel
pulls me back,
with its blond curls,
to the clip of poles
in thick water, crusted with the rind
of peeled fruit,
the crack of mainland guns
collecting
like the sough of mosquitoes
after monsoon.

Children sell painted boxes
and mangoes cut like clowns' lips,
slewing through lotus flats
as night drops down
tight as an outgrown bangle.

On land ankle chain beads
and skull caps
bake on tin trays,
the pipefires from hookahs
and mint tea
steam.
Curfew creeps up
like dark cats.
We hardly know its scratch.

The ladies used to sit here
under parasols
in white cottons
sampling the summer winds
rolled from the Indus rocks

to the lake,
pressing orchid petals
and washing their hair
in perfumed tea.

now where we sit,
wood pared off the summer boats
like honey,
drinking tea with ghee
as the little girl floats by
her hair strung with flowers
selling marigold garlands
and bags of henna.

We didn't notice nightfall either,
when the first man cut curfew.
This was the place we came
for rest and cool
and the lap of lake
on hot sandalwood,
the swoon of jasmine.

He was walking home late
when guncracks threw him
where donkey pats
drew flies
and the dust dragged red
and his cap, once white
as sahib teeth,
was kicked under a cow's hoof,
and never retrieved.

RALPH J. MILLS, JR.

10/93

what memory
of clouds
the trees part-
way
unsleeved –

a dry
day, heat'll be
back up awhile
a
while
these early
brief gusts
working higher –
third of
a moon straight
over me
white as any
scratched stone
rim
powdering
in dawn's
blue vapor –

A LITTLE/SUN

a little
sun
touches this
locust,
yellow birch
in curls –

one mourning
dove flutes,
repeats
out of back-
yard trees

: the sky
changes – lunar
grey of dove's
head,
feathers,
its "diagnostic"
whistling wings –

JIM STEVENS

MOOSE

They are older than the deer,
their movements slower,
a tempo somehow as primitive
as the shape of their heavy heads,
as the unmeasured passage of the sun
along the arch of heaven.

The white-tailed deer are creatures
of the moment, restless, insecure,
speeding across the evening fields
like quicksilver, and as quickly
taking flight back to the shelter
of the nearby poplars, their lives
controlled by every sound
and sight and smell coming from
a world outside themselves.

The moose are different,
listening to a low-pitched voice
deep inside their hides,
they stand like solid mysteries
alone or in two's or three's
black against the snow.

At times you see them lying there
oblivious, the great ears
of the cows projecting upwards
like the flight of owls
hunting in the night

the ears of the bull dwarfed
by his massive antlers, heavy
with the number of his years.

At times you see them getting up,
a slow unfolding of their bones,
and then a shake to rid themselves
of snow and the shape of lying down.

And then you watch them taking their leave,
their long legs striding in a walk
that is more like standing still
or like the eon drift of continents
than walking, until somehow they are gone,
disappearing in their past.

CHET COREY

FIELDS OF MEMORY

1
Perhaps they have never sat so long
as on these strands of wire
they bend down, unaware of twists
of gossip within, the slip
of a marriage into an affair,
the child calling from college,
confused and coming home.

These flocking grackles, waiting
to take to fields further south –
how reluctant they seem,
as if the voices within these wires
had penetrated their sure-toed grip,
redoubled the weight of their bodies.

2
They could be mistaken for mourners
at a curbside, gathered to watch
for a riderless horse and caisson,
fatherless children –
the face behind the veil.

A few lift off, only to return.
And then, as at the passing
of the colors, the beating of wings.

3
When I walk again this gravel road,
I will not recall on which they sat,
will settle for the approximate.

I doubt that even they will recollect
these hours of diminished light
should they return with offspring
to flock above these combined fields,
wait for their dark nation to regroup.

They will be like the grandfathers
and fathers returning with generations
of children, confused by all the bright
cold concrete of a nation's capitol,
who must settle for the approximate –
remember a storefront, a bank of trees,
say that it was about here we sat,
with your mothers and your grandmothers,
beside a quiet Potomac and wept.

NEIGHBORS

The farmer on the south side of the road
hopes in the Contract for America,
learns to use the Internet,
studies the marketshare in China.

The farmer on the north side of the road
wonders why he never thought to mix
ammonium nitrate with fuel oil –
blow the whole damn place to kingdom come.

Both farmers wait for better weather.

CROSSING NEBRASKA

1
The black water
of winter,
like a window out
in a farmhouse.

Snow melt
on the turned fields:
weathered board,
white once as birch.

2
The open creeks,
ditches and fieldrows:
wet black
as the trunks of oaks –
singular, secure.

More mirror like
because of overcast.

And all the dead grass.

3
The sacred is what
is set aside.

Darkness reflected up,
not down.

4
An electric cross
blinks on

(automatically,
every night)

above the doorway of
an Evangelical church

on ground no good
for plow or pasture.

5
Black water
wherever it is found
reflects back up
what refuses,
is not ready to fall.

Telephone pole
and wire.

Woods,
overcast sky.

6
I am startled
by standing water
at a crossroad

as if it were
a car about to strike.
As if I had read
my own name on a mailbox.

Like listening to opera
on the radio
and understanding
none of it,
nor needing to.

7
I want to walk
over to it
and to see my face.

I want to see
the bright stone a
star casts down,

ripples of light
traded
back and forth
between the small hands
of waves.

DAKOTA CINQUAIN #2

Cloud swept,
prairie grasses
bend leaf and seedy heads
as if Mecca were the Black Hills.
Wakan!

THE COMING ON OF WINTER

1
Barns ride out the halogen night
like Russian barges outbound from Duluth,
arks of wheat rocking through fog
above the mountain crags of Lake Superior.

2
The screen door of an abandoned farm
knocks like a beggar in a parable,
announces to neighbors how another Noah
got up one night to change the fuzzy channel
on the TV set and heard a voice go hard
against all he had thought was gain.

3
Someone drove over, looked through windows
of empty rooms of carpet, one of linoleum,
a two-burner stove and the avocado Frigidaire.

Within a week, whoever came back in the night,
called it once by name, then shot the barking dog.

4
Some say he had a plan. Any banker could have seen
it coming sure as Christ. Others say it was his wife.

No one has thought to fix the hinge,
to shoot the other off.

<u>*NANCY FREDERIKSEN*</u>

PETRARCHAN SONNET TO A LAWYER

Out from under your promissory notes
and the pledges of stock you had me draft,
where workload was never evenly halfed
and ridicule came with commas and quotes;

and away from the corner where anger floats
where setting things straight on your behalf
and dodging bullets became my craft –
another is now *the one who dotes*,

who notices and notes the patterns of scorn.
Torn from the familiar I longed to linger
but old cards were shuffled, a new game borne.
Out from under the point of your finger
the point of my own determines my course.
The full measure of difference is being the source.

NICKIE J. GUNSTROM

A PUBLIC LIFE

He's hiding again. I can't find him.
I thought he'd gotten over that.
Maybe he's under the bed. I'll look.
Not there? Look under our bed.
What about the closet? Remember how he . . .
Not there. I'll check the other closets.
See if he's in the basement, would you?
What's that noise?
It's outside, sounds like people cheering.
Oh, come look. Isn't that he in the center?
Yes, he's standing on top of the garden wall.
It's looks like he's giving a speech.
Well, good. they seem to like it.
It's about time, don't you think?

In Flanders Field
DC '00

RIGHT ON DOWN

By Chester G. Anderson

Henry Augustus Johnson, doctor of philosophy and professor of literature, was annoyed. He swerved his 1953 Plymouth into the parking lot next to the tavern and slammed on the brakes. It was a warm night in May, 1959. He reached for the paperback volume of Robert Frost's poems on the seat beside him and stepped out onto the parking lot. As he crossed the lot towards the lighted screen door, he caught himself humming the romantic strains of "Laura" still turning on the tavern jukebox fourteen years after the war. He frowned at this residue of what he viewed as a phony youth. Then he scowled at the affected repudiation which had made him frown.

"Goddamn it," he thought. "If I want to hum 'Laura,' I'll hum it!" But he strode the last ten steps to the door in silence, his feet crunching hard on the gravel of the lot.

Henry was annoyed at his failure to persuade the tired school-teachers and housewives in his evening course at the college that the form or "structure" of a poem is more important than its subject. They had held out for pasture springs and birch trees, he for the *shape* of feelings and thoughts: for the pattern of words which ordered part to part. Not that the form and subject could be separated, he had told them more than once. The form *is* the meaning. He was not always sure what he meant by this, but he had seen the idea expressed by Ernst Cassirer and Suzanne Langer, and he believed.

He thought that he might cool his annoyance by drinking a few beers and reading some of Frost's poems before going home. Frost's were the only poems he had with him. He wished that they were Yeats's or Stevens's.

Henry noticed as he entered the barroom that it was working-class, full of smoke and the smell of stale beer. The odors reminded him of certain lines that T. S. Eliot had imitated from Laforge in 1917. The smoke, his nostrils told him, was both pipe and cigarette – a mixture not uncommon in air-conditioned cocktail lounges. It made him feel comfortably close to the people. The bartender, a red-faced, overweight man in his middle thirties, was playing duckpins with three neighborhood regulars. Four or five other men were gathered around the undersized alley, drinking beer and kibitzing on the game. They glanced up as Henry entered, with the looks of mildly hostile indifference which Henry had often noticed were reserved in blue-collar taverns for strangers wearing suits and white shirts and neckties. The bartender threw a strike as Henry walked towards a stool at the short side of the L-shaped bar, but he did not hurry over to serve him.

Henry perched on the stool and opened the book. By the dim light which came through the cheap shade of a pin-up lamp over the bourbon, he noticed the woman. A striking woman, maybe beautiful, her face looked as cruel as that of Diana, the huntress. She was sitting on a stool behind the bar smoking a cigarette in a black holder and half closing her long black lashes to protect her eyes from the smoke. Or was that why? The adverb *seductively* shaped itself slowly in Henry's mind. She looked, he thought, like Eustacia Vye transplanted from Egdon Heath to a hothouse where all she had to do was to sit and grow beautiful. Her hair was as black as Rowena's and she had skin as soft and white and fine-grained as a camilla petal – or even of Camille herself. She wore a black silk sheath that fit tight over her full breasts and just barely gave her room to cross one lovely leg over the other in a silksoft movement that made Henry think of fierce women in novels by Laclos.

He allowed his fancy to conjure scenes from Henry Miller as she crossed her legs again. His eyes moved down her wide hips and along the curve of her leg all the way to the page open before him. The fat bartender indolently waited to take another turn at the duckpins before he came around the bar to serve Henry. With the lazy skill born of long practice he had thrown another perfect strike. He walked past the beautiful woman without a word or a look, and for a moment Henry had the agonizing feeling he might be her husband.

"What'll you have?" the bartender asked as he gave the bar in front of Henry a swipe with the bar rag.

"I'd like a beer – a bottle of *Miller's*, if you don't mind." Henry hoped that his last phrase did not sound condescending. He should have had a draft beer.

The bartender did not reply. He opened the cooler, took out a bottle of *Miller's* and reached for a glass from the neat row in front of the mirror.

"What are you reading?" he asked as he set the beer in front of Henry.

"A poem by Robert Frost," Henry said.

The bartender wiped his fat hands on his apron and gazed curiously at Henry. His small blue eyes were bleary and vague, set deep in his porcine face. His look did not seem to be the look of an enemy. His eyes were dimly seeking, perhaps, unaccustomed paths of communication. Frustrated in their search, they skewed off. He let his apron drop from his stubby white fingers and went round the bar again to take his turn at the duckpins. Henry carefully poured his glass full of beer and relished the first cool sip. He returned to his reading, though he could not summon the kind of attention which, he knew, even the easy lines of Frost demand. From the corner of his eye, he noticed that the bartender had thrown another strike and was approaching him on the customers' side of the bar.

"I've read some of Robert Frost's poems," the bartender said.

"Oh, have you?" Henry said. For a moment, a sardonic plan occurred to him of reciting one of the maple-sugar poems to the dull man before him – "I'm going down to clean the pasture spring" or "When I see birches bend to left and right" – and then proving, with the brilliant rapier-play of insight and example which he managed on his best nights in the classroom, that it is the form, not the subject, which makes even second-rate poems affect the dullest minds. Although he might not penetrate the viscid swamp of the man's sensibilities, Guinevere across the bar might appreciate his gestures and cast her favor towards him on the jousting field of the aesthetic judgment.

"Yeah. No, no! I don't mean Robert Frost. Who's some other Robert that writes poems? Robert . . .ah . . . ."

The bartender's face showed the strain of his mind as it fumbled for the misplaced name. With relief he returned to the game at the impatient call of his comrades. He rolled a bad three-two split and picked up only one pin on his second skim of the silver disk down the alley. He came around the bar and served Henry another beer. The bewilderment was still on his face.

"Robert – oh, dammit, it's right on the tip of my tongue."

"Graves?" Henry suggested. "Or Lowell? Bly? Creeley?" He glanced at the woman to see if her face had registered any pleasure at the sight of this academic cruelty. None was registered. The face was as impassive as the mask of a prostitute in a Japanese play.

"Naw, not Brave! Robert – ah – about a saloon he wrote."

"Service!" said Henry.

A bunch of the boys were whooping it up
In the Malamute saloon.

"That's it! Robert Service. He's a helluva good poet."

"Well," Henry said, controlling the evil smile that twitched his lips, "opinion is divided in the schools. Have you – ?"

But before Henry could complete his sentence, the barman again returned to his game. He made a spare with a relaxed flourish and came back towards Henry's perch.

"You know what poem I really like, though?"

"No," Henry said. "What poem?"

"'In Flanders' Fields'," he said. "And you know why I like it?"

"No," Henry said. "Why?"

Henry's mind pitched back thirty years and a thousand miles westward to his boyhood home in Wisconsin, where he was surprised to find the warm sun of late spring still shining in patterns on the dark green grass of Glen Park Cemetery and glinting from the brass trombones and tubas of the high school band and gleaming on the barrels of the Springfield rifles which the national guardsmen held at parade rest, ready to shoot the volleys at the end of the ceremony, while up on the temporary platform, Judge Thompson sat sleepily in his white sharkskin suit – the only white suit in town – his broadbrimmed Panama with the narrow blue band carefully placed beneath the folding chair on which he sat, having already delivered his Memorial Day speech –

> *. . .the great war which we, the living,*
> *must make the war to end all wars by*
> *keeping faith with those dear, departed*
> *sons of our fair town who fell in battle*
> *to make the world safe for democracy*
> *and who now sleep in foreign fields . . .*

– now listening half-attentively to the voice of Romaire Zorn, champion high-school debater:

> *In Flanders' Fields the poppies blow*
> *Between the crosses, row on row,*
> *That mark our place . . .*

a handsome boy, his black hair slicked down with pomade, his dark skin scrubbed shiny with soap and water, brother to Maja, Henry's dark childhood love, son of the only blacksmith in town, by whose cheery forge only yesterday Henry had sat on a bench with Maja, innocent of Haephestus and Athena, watching the sparks fly from the horseshoe Mr. Zorn pounded on the anvil, watching the thick black hair, curly with sweat, on old Zorn's muscular forearm as he held the shoe with the pincers and plunged it into the water cask, hearing the impatient stamp of the horse's unshod hoof on the plank floor, smelling the acrid coalsmoke and still moist, somehow rectangular droppings of the horse.

"You want to know why I like it?" the bartender asked again.

"Why?"

The bartender raised his heavy right hand into the air and with the thick index finger described a straight horizontal line about eighteen inches long.

"I like the way it starts up here – 'In Flanders Fields,'" he said, again writing the line on the air. "It starts up here and comes right on down – 'The poppies blow.'"

As he announced the second line, his finger wrote again, about a foot below and parallel to the first line, which still hung there, Henry thought, in the smoky air. In spite of the cries of his friends, telling him that he was holding up the game, the bartender repeated his entire performance, including the two lines, one above the other, drawn on the blue air. The demands of his comrades became agitated, slightly annoyed. His face was peaceful, however, almost ecstatic as he said the two lines for the second time.

"Another beer?" he asked.

"No, thank you," Henry said. "I'd better be moving along."

"Nice talking to you," the bartender said. "Do you see what I mean about that poem?"

"I think I do," Henry said. "It's a very interesting theory."

The woman got up and walked towards the jukebox. Her breasts jiggled from her soundless laughter.

"You're a real pisser, Joe," she said to the bartender. "A real pisser!" She dropped a dime into the jukebox and "Laura" began on a flat note as the record picked up speed.

As the professor walked towards the door, Joe was addressing the sawdust-covered alley. He shouted over the noise of the jukebox: “It starts up there, and comes right on down!”

Henry shoved the screendoor open and stepped into the evening. He heard all ten pins drop on Joe’s first roll.

ROBLEY WILSON

THE CROWS AT DAWN

If you have quarreled with the woman
you love, the crows indict you.
Call, call her, they chorus, *confess*,

as if guilt heals, as if contrition
were an answer, as if a clapping
of tongues, *because I*, makes it up.

Every dawn they count, cross,
discuss, who have never cried down
a soft apology in their lives.

ALLEN HAMILTON BATES

FOR JON AND KATRINA

O even exiled gods or those extinct
Would bless the sweet conjunction of these hearts.
This pair, despite the poisoned oceans, linked
Their limbs, their souls, and all their precious parts.

Against the dark, against the dirt, they join –
Fond sentinels that guard the other's sleep.
No death nor debt shall tarnish love's bright coin
Nor doubt amend such vows as gallants keep.

Yes, taken all in all, let's name them brave
Who dare the ozone's rent and urban crime –
For only stalwart love outwits the grave
Though odds say shrewdest money bets on time.

Believe, dear duo please, this prescient verse –
You shall thrive better though the world grow worse.

TO JOHN D'AMBRISI

On any dark morning
sleep's truant
you stalked your own house
like a nervous burglar
looking not for silver
but for something to fix.

Food was your love's currency
and dearest measure –
you paid the coin of wheat and sauces
baked to the point of alizarin
rich and crusty as old dried blood.

In the vivid family
where clowns are for hire
and the troupers are lauded
for their guises,
you were the real idol
of matinees.

I wished for you
the bandstand
the microphone
the network
you deserved
and the portrait and table at Sardi's.

According to your son
you seldom finished a book
but prized them more
than Persian scholars could

as you subdued them with your fingers
stared at their pages
as you did the face of your wife.

Now you are with the stars
and crooners you adored
and praised so hugely
at their passing.

Past protection from the bathtub
where you sought safety from the war
now you have the stillness
that eluded you.

3 July 1995

ROME, 1982

The Roman starlings
flexing themselves in the morning
driving and swooping
across our long window
abrupt like police whistles.

Think if one took a turn
like a terrorist
and entered our room!

how animated
it would become —
like me
when I hear of old lovers.

GEORGE.T. WRIGHT

SAMLA, 1967

A carful of questions, jokes, gripes, witty asides,
tossed up for two-hundred miles to Atlanta.
One – "highly articulate" – sprinkles his syntax with curse words;
one sulks with a laugh; one leaves his glasses behind
at a roadside cafe.

The weather is blue, Atlanta jammed, we collect
our hotels and dismiss our car. At lunch
John Tinkler appears, invites, dematerializes.
And then old faces, older this year, begin
their smiling, bare-child tramp

across my tearing page. The papers are all too long,
the people are all too far. Why is everyone grinning?
Crazed by the yellow light that crisps our faces,
revulsion like a gangster, fatigue like a film
gun us all down.

Or so it seems to me who absconds for a nap
in a poisonous mood and wakes wary but clear.
Evening cools, disperses veils and voices.
Under smoked scotch, the pieces for a while are radiant
and just where I put them.

But the morning light, highly articulate, smiles
its void at my crowded, questioning eyes. Atlanta,
empowered by sleep, cashes our next year's handshakes.
Schooled, in the sludge of noon we scatter home
to pick up fogged-up lives and glasses.

DISTANT COUSINS

The snow isn't worried.
Flakes like swarming bees beat about the gaslight,
small white things dropped out of the night,
We come from different families.

Mother of snow, my life,
grow next to this beautiful child, take on its
color and softness before it folds its
water and leaves us.

This trunk, my heart,
is almost always already halfway filled
with poor relations. Bring me to my knees.
Come through the glass, snow, muffle and dance me.

MAURA STANTON

ICEMAN

The T.V. camera pans across a body
hikers found beneath a melting glacier.
Five thousand years ago this lake dweller
climbed the mountain above his village
just like I do every summer, and his goal
wasn't commerce, some trade in flint,
as the commentator insists, it was
simply a beautiful day when he set out
and the mysterious peaks drew him up.
Caught in a snowstorm, he burrowed down
into a crevice where he died from cold.
Now two countries claim his remains.
Though his penis and scrotum are missing
after picks freed him from the ice,
he's a prize of Neolithic chemicals.
I like his leather pouch of sloeberries
for they look like the blueberries bagged
inside my own freezer, and his unstrung bow
suggests he wasn't going too far, he meant
to turn back at every step, but the view
ravished him, and he followed the goat path
higher and higher with untipped arrows
and a useless bow, until the clouds moved
swiftly across the glittering blue limestone,
and he shivered, looked back. Now we see
he had charcoal tattoos striping his back
and knees, grass stuffed into his shoes
of sewn leather, and two dried mushrooms
hanging from a string. Is this the afterlife?
One man survives his tribe and family
keeping his human shape, even his skin,

though his eye jelly's gone, and his dreams
have evaporated from the frozen brain
sliced under the microscope. The star
that once exploded to make him, still shines,
for his body protein emits radiation,
just a little, but enough to date him.
When I turn off the set, I hear the wind
clicking sleet against the windowpanes.
In six months I'll walk the Iceman's trails
into the Alps, where the heart melts,
and if I only believed in five thousand years
to come, I would prepare to arrive there.
I'd choose an object, and I'd drop it
into the crevice of a deep, rippled glacier –
something scribbled down in my own writing
or a ring with my name inside for easy fame.

HANDWRITING

My sleeve soaked by the automatic spray
Misting the curly endive, my wire cart
Wedged by the potato bin, I'm puzzling
Over my own grocery list. Reams and silk
For supper? Pest food? Some tango chips,
A bottle of red wave? I think my brain
Needs other food than what my stomach craves,
And twists my hand into this messy scrawl –
Why waste time on useful cheese and rye
When I could search the aisles for chirps
In cellophane bags, buy loaves of rhyme bread,
Every slice exact? Once in grade school
I let my handwriting shrink, almost vanish.
No one but me could read the faint squiggles
Floating above blue lines of tablet paper.
At first I just wrote tiny, taking care
To shape each miniature letter perfectly,
But when I realized the teacher couldn't read
My homework answers in such little script,
(WRITE BIGGER! she scrawled across the top)
I faked whole lines, giving the illusion
Of sense with all my tiny dots and spirals.
Why? I don't know. I knew the answers.
"Can you read this?" she asked once, pointing
And I did, extemporizing, so that
My homework counted. That's when she gave me
A wooden ruler, and forced me to write
So all my letters fit a measured height.
Glancing now at my list, I see I do
Write large – the lesson stuck – but no more

Clearly than before. Shall I put margins
On my toast, add cruelty to salads,
Drink orange joy? As I dig for blueberries

In the frozen food bin, turning up bags
Of rhubarb and black cherries, my fingers
Burn with frost, searching for something new
On sale today, maybe ziz-zags of lightning
Some merchant harvested with a thousand kites
And trucked to my town, cubed, still radiant.

DENNIS SALEH

TEMPLE SALE

Temple Sale! Temple Sale! Closing for eternity! Lost our peace! Gods, gods, gods! We got 'em! Boatloads, bargeloads, galleyloads! More than two thousand different gods to choose from! Everything goes! All sizes, shapes, colors, styles! Stacked to the temple top, and coming out the columns! You won't believe your eyes! Your friends won't believe the deal you make! Nothing down! Instant credit approval! Eternal installment plan! You make the deal, we make up the difference! Our loss, your gain! Once in a lifetime opportunity! Don't miss out! Dealers welcome! Bring the young ones! Live ritual, live ceremony, live sacrifice! Last chance! Get here before they're gone! When was the last time you had a new god? Don't you deserve a new god today? Hurry down! Open late! Near river, look for sails!

THE CREATION

The universe is not completed, we know, and this is no clearer than in the Spring, when everything begins all over again. Contrary to modern ecclesiastical thought, God did not rest on the seventh day, but on that day created metaphor, and we all know what that is for, for on the eighth day he created art. Now, by contemporary reckoning, this would make it Monday. This day, four angels came to God while he was creating, each with a question. The first asked God why he was creating, the second asked God how he was able to create, and the third asked if he could have the creation when it was finished. But the fourth angel asked God if he could help, and this was the angel of art. And yes, Tuesday, after having created art, God did rest. After art, everything else would create itself. After art, even dirt is just something misplaced. Since that time, only God and artists have worked on Sundays.

A TO Z

Actor, the Thessalian hero, once wrote a play which accused Zeus of seducing Actor's great-grandmother, Cleitos, disguised as an ant. It is Cleitos who said, "Even an ant is the beginning of a new universe." Zeus tried to hush the whole thing up, and cursed Actor. Though his name would live ever after because of the scandalous affair, nothing real would ever be known about him, thus became that nature of fame, Actor's legacy. Actor's descendant, Aeacus, claimed a boon in redress, and for him, Zeus changed the ants of the island of Aegina into men. Aeacus also said, "Even an ant is the beginning of a new universe." From this tale we learn that any story with both an "A" and a "Z" in it is metaphorical. The only question is, what it is not about.

PURPLE WORDS

Purple words. A purple world. Brimming, rimful. Peacock. Coral. Anemone. Sea shawl. Adder tongue. Entrails. Sap. Resin. Fig purple, purple-stemmed. Moss purple. Dank purple. Buried purple. Purple moiré. Placenta of the day, and night, placenta of time, born out of eternity. Purple bloom of time. Eclipse. Blood of noon. Purple wind. Purple sail of mortality. Time darkened by use. Conclusion. Exhaustion. Old blood. Sodden. Purple premonition, shadow of the future, memory forecalled of death. Purple breath of an expiring goddess. Purple ichor. Purple from the blood of words. Blood of gloom. Purple is the blood of blue. The shadow of red. Labia purpura, purple-lipped. Purple mien. Purple thrall. Purple trance. Man's envy is green, some say, but Set's envy was purple, enraged, colored by his lust, gorged. Purple spit, Set's saliva. Purple spite, Set's gown. Purple spurt of false words: purple manqué. The purple flies of Set's mischief. Purple torment. Purple faience. Ebony purple. Ethiopian purple. Purple reign. Throne purple. Tomb purple. Moon purple. Pharaoh's root. Pharaoh's rancor.

SUSAN McCLEAN

THE SHARK AT THE AQUARIUM

I was fourteen when I learned about the food chain
At the shark tank of the Vancouver Aquarium.
I had seen fish in tanks before, but none
This large. Its flat eyes seemed not to see me
As it glided past, looking for prey.
A small crowd watched it, mesmerized by
Menace, and the man in front of me
Leaned back against me, hands behind his back,
His fingers writhing against my crotch
Like the tentacles of sea anemones.

I backed away, embarrassed, went to stand
Before another tank. This time he pressed
Against me from behind, shifting his weight
Slowly to rub against me. I glanced back.
In the blue glow, his eyes stared straight ahead
As if he didn't see me. My heart pounding,
I squeezed out of the crowd and rushed away
Through the blue-green semi-darkness, looking for
My parents, who told me not to make things up
And not to wander off. I had not known
Till then that I was part of the food chain.

The shark is not malicious. He has needs.
The smaller fish just look like food to him.

AERIALIST

I walk a fine line, a tension span
Between opposite poles. The line cannot
Be taut; it must have give in it to forgive
The misplaced foot, but not enough to yaw
And wobble at each step. The crowd below
Watches me hungrily. An empty line
Is common as telephones; what draws the eye
Is the body poised above nothing, the awful pause
As it staggers and recovers, the willed pose
Of nonchalance, the gravity of the position.

REBELLION

The door on which my father pounds
Jumps in its frame like the pulse in my throat.
I am almost thirteen and have done the unthinkable,
Tried to have the last word in an argument
By running to my room and locking the door –
Only to learn that I have no room,
That all the rooms are his.
He will cancel my birthday this year.
Many years later, I sit in another room.
Another door stands open,
Words rush through it onto a page,
And each of them counts,
Every
Last
Word.

HUNGER

Instead of writing a poem, I have baked you
This loaf of apricot-cinnamon bread. Eat it
While it is warm, while the cinnamon sugar,
Melted to a syrup, oozes from the slice.
It will taste of the mother or grandmother you had
Or wish you'd had, the love that expresses itself
Through comfort and delight. You may think
That I have done this for your love, for gratitude,
For a reputation as a good cook. The truth
Is that poets and cooks are always hungry,
Even after eating. We yearn for unknown flavors,
For the known flavors in new permutations.
Like God or DNA, we are testing out
The possible combinations. When the pink half-moon
Tilts low on the horizon, we want to bite it.

CHARLES EDWARD EATON

READING THE LEAVES

Have you sometimes wondered if autumn's fortune
Could be better told with tea leaves, reduced
In a cup, the sadness, the fire's soaring,
The ash that dreams an albino landscape? –
It is the rich imbuement that cannot last:
The leaf on the hand like a splayed birthmark,
The veins pulsing their fat caterpillars,
The jugular coursing with memories of wine,
The having tasted, taken in so much,
The threat of not quite metamorphic glut –
When will the death-wish settle in the cup? –
Come flexure, come twister, come rising wind.
See, the golden mounds shift like trembling graves,
The sudden dervish of a released spirit.
The gutters whisper from their cluttered lips,
Predict that the swamped car escapes in time,
While the leaf-sweeper swills its motley drink.
A worn and rusted man stares at the dregs,
Wants to be malleable, to be bent,
Folded over, hinged, cut into slivers,
In love with piecemeal prophecies –
I would need the thin membrane of the ox
Goldbeaters use for layering the leaves
To have enough to gild these many moods:
The sunset that lacquers its bloom on my skin,
The fruit that rolls over on its rotten spot,
The wine juice going brown in the scuppernong –
So I turn in the world's distribution –
Do not ask me the wish of tomorrow:
  I sway and swerve in the flair of the leaves.

THOMAS McCARTHY

HONEYMOON PORTRAIT

What survives is an image of you
as youth on the brink of some new distress.
Neither the raw carnivals of Paris
of *fin de siècle* ironworks break through

to allow for celebration. Your distant
look, your eyes that went dark with boredom,
constantly escape from the cheap bedroom
of tourist art. Your anecdotes rinse

the romantic hogwash out of moonlight.
Wait, who mentioned the moon?
Give the moon a break. The highly strung
Vietnamese exile has a perfect right

to paint the moon and dissolve the moon
to suit the purpose of her loaded brush.
What murderous B-26 crushed
her native studio and made her a Western

portrait painter? She chokes now in the lacquer
factory of Paris. She is one more displaced
woman, bombed out with her mother
from the Asian delta. The chalk she placed

to her lips was sulphurous with napalm.
Between you two there was a resonant mantra;
a prayer excluding men. You shared tourism
of the globe and the female body. I saw

the look of exile in her trapped eyes.
She caught the look of a honeymoon in you:
how no intelligent woman could subdue
the loss of territory that a marriage means.

SNOW

Cold palette of winter on the narrow lane.
I park the fat beige tube of car and walk.
Kate's hair, like a wayward streak of Titian,
cuts through the pure viridian of air.
We jump to avoid the soluble blue
of an Opel, a strong Prussian intruder.
Our hand link across the bismuth white
of packed snow. Without speech,
warm in the encrusted seal of her lips,
we catch the blue of a child hurrying indoors.
A nod of acknowledgment, a thumb raised,
delicate as camel-hair, she disappears.
Suddenly, the brilliant tincture of a child's laugh
from the euchrome of the cloakroom.

Daughter, your lips are too sore to kiss now;
your cool face, titanium white of inert snow.

LOVE MEDICINE

Sunlight falls on the April drinking vessel,
evening sunlight like an Australian pearl-shell.
A bumble-bee flops from its winter dream-time.
Persistent birdsong animates the fetus.
I watch the children at their ancient rites,
the ritual avoidance of brother and sister –
Kate determined to avoid the levirate,
Neil, with his kangaroo-skin headdress,
negotiates the tribal ochre of azaleas.

Old prams, tyres, shreds of earthenware,
are residue of the owners who once lived here,
dreaming their unfinished lease, their firesticks.
Remnants accumulate when I sink the spade,
while our own children go walkabout,
bound for the interior, full of love-magic.
We watch their heads disappear in the fresh
while the sun flings deadly stones of heat
light drunk with fragrance from their birth.

JARED CARTER

RAINCROW

Lost in the evening shadows now, you breathe
your strange sorrow – a pale lamp gleaming,
softly reclaimed again, among the leaves –

echo of long-forgotten hallways, wreathed
with faint perfume. I have heard you dreaming
lost in the evening shadows. Now you breathe

upon the mirror, and their faces show beneath
the stairway. I stand beside them, beaming,
softly reclaimed again among the leaves.

What is it that you place before us, sheathed
in darkness? What fragrant beaker teeming,
lost in the evening shadows? Now you breathe

your five notes, and the wind's reply seethes
through the branches; the twilight, streaming
softly, reclaimed again among the leaves,

gathers around us, and your song bequeaths
approaching rain, and solitude, and seeming.
Lost in the evening shadows now you breathe,
softly reclaimed again among the leaves.

GEORGE ROBERTS

THE GOOD FORGETTING

Each day Roger Waits Buffalo sits at the edge of the classroom . . . stays as far from the center of things as possible. He rarely speaks – and then, only in the quietest of voices, the shortest of sentences.

Like Elfriede's cat, he has his own manner of getting through the day. No amount of coaxing or bribing or training will alter his resolute way of placing empty fists on the desk. He never does writing assignments – list your favorite things, tell about your odd family members, make a guess at your future – only stares off into some white place while others dutifully scribble their journal entries.

One morning, almost to himself, he said how much he missed the open school on the reservation, then asked out loud, "What day is this?"

"Tuesday." "Tuesday," "Tuesday," everyone offered, surprised he asked for anything, and equally surprised at their need to answer.

"Tuesday . . .?" he nodded. "Tuesday . . . I thought it was Wednesday . . . Tuesday must have been a good day."

HOME VISITS

winter

The knob is missing from the front door of Andre's house. Only a small brass circle, a key plate, hints at how the door might open.

> We had to sell things . . .Christmas cards, stationery, magazine subscriptions, and worse, tickets to our plays . . . door to door.

After several knocks, an old woman, smiling, asks me in. A sleeping bag nailed to the doorway, blankets draped over windows, to hold out the cold.

> Each day our totals were entered on a big chart in the front of the room, and the glowing carrot of a prize for the highest sales dangled before us.

The grandmother smiles, says Andre and his mother are not home. Gone to the doctor. Andre must go with her, she tells me. Sometimes her daughter forgets the way home.

> There was that man, fumbling with his cane and his tiny coin purse, bought a play ticket from me . . . I held it out to him and he said, "Keep it. I'm too old and sick to leave the house."

I am standing in the middle of the living room as the floor turns to quicksand. My voice, a hundred miles away, is saying "Andre has missed some school, has some assignments to make up . . . "

"I'll be sure to tell his mother," the grandmother says, her smile never changing, her cloudy eyes never flinching.

THE FORGOTTEN JACKET

Michelle has wandered out of class and left her coat again. It hangs on the back of her chair, blue and orange and dirty around the cuffs, like the spirit of a dead grandmother hovering above its own fresh grave. One sleeve touches the floor, the other turns in upon itself, asking "Who, me?" Scuffed snow where the family stood, mute, for the service. Only the silence of the rest of time and the creaking of trees in the wind comfort the lonely grandmother now.

And Michelle . . . . fogs through her classes, not missing her coat, or the pencils, lunch money, kleenex in the pocket. She has not slept well for nights. Her parents are fighting and her room does not have a door.

At the end of the day, she begins to cry. "I've lost my jacket," she sobs. "It's too cold to go home without it."

"There, there," comforts her teacher. "Your grandmother would understand . . . ."

STEVEN STROMME

SIX HAIKU

the geese keep coming
as we tremble, heads bowed
Saskatchewan

shadows of snow geese
drift over my sleeping son . . .
his first hunting trip

snow geese
swirl shyly overhead . . .
our Cree guide pleads

a blur of timber wolves
beneath the shimmering tamaracks –
moose calf chest deep in snow

lone goose
turning to my call
my son's "Let's not shoot . . . ."

hen mallard
preening a shattered wing
under a hunter's moon

KATE HALLETT DAYTON

SUMMER LIGHT, LOST

I see a lone egret walking the weeds away from a pond surrounded by grassland. Out of place. Clearly searching, her head shoots out in several directions, but she continues to move inland. I, too, wander through tall grass, drive the back roads to work.

In fall, the egrets are on the edge of the pond and on my mind. I watch their rhythmic movement and wonder how to keep them here. In late October I search the roadside ponds and marshes for their white, curved bodies, but there are none. No backs toward me, nor heads buried along the length of their bodies. A spot of white in a tree draws my eye, but wafts from the limb, a white plastic bag, caught.

Egrets do not cross my path, but leave silently. Not like the geese in a noisy arrow flight. I look to the sky, mottled with cirrus clouds like hundreds of white ghosts, suspended.

KARLA HAMMOND

INTIMATIONS OF A FEELING

for P.S.B.

It isn't that I am
without song, to
tell you, only words;

forgetting this arrival
treating it always
in the present tense

listen: I like you
this time I like you
& that has come to mean

something graver, lighter
than the laying on of hands,
the intensity of sex;

friend, that melody is finer,
rarer, than loving or
the saying of such words.

VERMONT JULY

Three months of heat. The air turns
dust. Discs of light circle the drive,
dye the grass a brassy jade. In
the shadows of porch beams, stillness

deepens. At my side, Molly Taber
wags her chin in sleep. Fingers
clasp a sweat-clad waist, her belly
stretched by years of appetite

and birthing. Memory like summer
recaptures season, when she dreams
of other Julys: the watering hole,
berries ripening in their sheathes,

the rain locked away, sudden tempers of
rain, land – a sluice – taking it up,
holding it in. After cleansing, the garden
revived; flowers, selves, no longer thirsting.

W. R. MOSES

AUTUMN ANTINOMY

The Hunter's Moon is in the sky.
I shall not go hunting.
Those I might shoot are as much entitled
to a full life span as I.

Yet I am disquieted.
I ache to go out and kill.
I wonder – can I blame this Hunter's Moon lust
On hunters, dead

Or alive, who bloodily smiled at the Moon
And knew it signaled their season
And knew no ethical clogging
And knew that as soon

As day came, they would be weaponed and away?
Consider – those stares at the disc of blood –
Don't they rebound, come back
With the moon-image mirrored in the eye

Of the gazer? What if, through some time-space mix-up,
What comes back to me
Isn't the kill-not stare I sent,
But a happy one darted up

By a hunting-gathering man in the moonlight
Or someone living now
Who would see the wing collapse, the blood on the fur,
With uncomplicated delight?

PRESENT/PAST

I don't like to be bullied by linear time . . . .

I shall go to a house in the woods. It's now rather
A wreck, partly burned, partly gale stripped,
Most of the floor boards too rotten to risk treading.
Yet some mighty, stronger-than-time ability
Will recover what's vanished, put it again together,

And a homely, pleasant, might-have-been cousin will gather
Her face in a smile of greeting. We'll chat a bit
Of homely matters. Before long I'll go and bring her
Fish from the nearby pond. Tomorrow she'll bake me
Coffee cake for breakfast. A bird will sing from a cedar.

PAST/PRESENT

"Hey, let's go fishing! Let's go to Top Side!"
So scramble round. A long streetcar ride.
Then seven miles (wasn't it?) of railway track.
A rattler's buzz. But when we circled back
(Ever so cautiously) we couldn't find
Any rattler. Lunch. But – we had left behind,
At home, the can opener for the bean can.
Well, one needn't be a very inventive man
To handle that: just pound with a sharp stone.
A very good day: all grin, never a groan.

Subjective time, Oh subjective time –
Isn't it the devil? It just won't climb
Around the objective dial at objective speed.
To try that trip now, what would we need?
Oh, not wheel chairs literally. But we couldn't go
That far – that's certain. And I don't even know
Whether you're alive, my adolescent friend.
Yet it swells in me, the feeling you might send
That call again, tomorrow, not to be denied:
"Hey, let's go fishing! Let's go to Top Side!"

ROBERT COUTEAU

AT VILLAGE ST. PAUL IN THE MARAIS

The best time with you for me
was when I'd arrived unbidden at midnight
and you'd drunk so much champagne
your head was sparkling
and your unhesitating womb clenched me
in its deep and relaxed manner
and you blurting
oui . . . .oui . . ..oui
and I said o.k. o.k.
o.k. *d'accord*!
shouting about
satisfactions that left us
dumb.

I still remember your sprightly bed
your window framing the great gray
dome of St. Catherine's Cathedral
the winding cubist courtyards of
St. Paul and the ancient Roman
wall where the men played
pétanque in the orange dust
while I stared at them from overhead
still shocked to gaze up at clouds watery
blue and brooding: How did I ever
make it here actually living my days
in Paris I remember every
detail but I don't
remember your
name.

August, 1990

BARON WORMSER

ALLEGORY

Happiness comes over to the house
    and brings her friends with her
    in her big Chev station wagon.
    It needs new shocks. The paint job
    is called "Spring Blue."

Alacrity licks all the crumbs off her plate
    and applauds the electric lights.
Pleasure strokes the cat.
Contentment hums show tunes and watches
    the dust settle.
Orgasm is unruly.
Civility murmurs assent.
Gaiety does handstands and paints her toenails.
Sanguine deftly unfolds the hopes of the new administration.
    Democracy is messy but better than
    anything else, she avers.
Savor kisses the condiments, particularly the relishes.

When they leave, I got out to buy a newspaper.
I'm whistling some Duke Ellington and I've got on
    my soft worn corduroy baseball cap.
The guy who gives me change with my Lifesavers and
    lottery ticket asks me what's up.
Joy, I say. I love her. She's berserk.

STRANGERS

Around the time of the month
In the warm weather
When there was no or little moon
My mother's voice would assume
An unusual urgency.
"We need to drive beyond the lights,"
She'd say as she searched
For her customarily misplaced keys.

My sister and I got into
The two-tone Ford Fairlane
And after a half-hour we
Had left incipient suburbia
Behind. My mother's driving-
The-car-humming had settled into

A modest soprano that
Wandered through the hit parade
Of 1941, now brassy,
Now wistful, now jaunty.

She pulled over on some
Dirt road and we got out.
The air was rich and spectral.
You could smell the fields, cows,
Soil, woods. We walked

Carefully, pausing now and then
To look up at the stars
Whose names we didn't know.
We were city people and they
Were amazing strangers.

We marveled and my sister and I
Sang along as best we could.
No houses or stores or street lights.
It was dark in the country and
It felt buoyantly and quietly right.

IN THE BANKRUPT HOUR: SAIGON, 1975

In the bankrupt hour
   Diplomat gravity
Lolls in a lizard sun.
   No simpering remorse –

It's what the flacks call
   "A clean conscience":
Mobile, press-briefed,
   And blown dry.

In the bankrupt hour
   Admissions
Of irritated principle
   Caress the hues

Of sincerity. Death
   Has made too many demands.
History needs some room to breathe.
   The last helicopter

Winds up from the embassy
   Roof into the Protestant
Sky. A gardener, a bookkeeper,
   A mistress, a low-level

Informer, an errand boy, a cook
   All look up wonderingly.
They knew this was coming
   Is what they say.

They turn towards their
   Provisional homes.
A dusky wind rises,
   The brisk flags are stones.

ALISON McGHEE

A PLACE THAT WANTS ONLY TO TAKE YOU

away from everything you know
into everything that was known.
You and your sisters, clutching berry boxes.
Brambles next to the pond, canes yearning over the creek.
Blackberries, thick tapered bodies
like bumble bees, darker than blue.
Work your way down the creek without knowing.
Drift away from this sister and that one.
Find your way into the heart of the patch.
This is where you are – a still summer day.
Your hair red-brown silk,
drifting waistward.
Sweet tang of berries
on your tongue.
Drone of insects.
Beat of sun.
Faraway days.

JOHN MITCHELL

IN OLD MEXICO

The air must be just about
 As God intended, mornings
Reminiscent of tequila
And beer sipped the night
Before, a kiss on the beach
Vaguely stale compared
To whiskey and the rising sun.
The belly with its golden hairs
Likes itself between
Almost empty and nearly full
Of avocado and black beans.
Imagination wasn't meant
To be non-human and so we
Who aspire to be something
More than a crushed can
Like to liken ourselves
To the mirrors in our brains.
If we could see our hands
As obsidian with ripple flaking
We'd like to cut one another
To see whose heart would bleed.

SUSAN YUZNA

SHAKESPEARE'S SISTER

After my first public poetry
reading, at a bookstore
in Iowa City, a Professor from the Workshop
said to me, *You were charming*.
I pondered this remark
though flushed with wine, I'll admit.
(I was nervous,
dragged into it . . .)
Does he mean I'm not good?

It was then
I noticed the woman
standing much too close,
her pale blue eyes
locked on my face.
I tried stepping back
but there was a pillar, or wall,
behind me. She was what
I then considered old –
thirties or forties.
Her name, I forgot or never knew.

She spoke suddenly.
You write for them,
and she waved her arm
in a slow arc
over the heads of an audience

mostly male
and mostly Workshop –
Not for us.
She turned and left.

Only now, as I sit
at this basement desk
with the echo of her single sentence
come bouncing down the years,
do I know
why she built a fire
in the Visiting Lecturer's
back yard, and dancing
around it, pulled
off her clothes.

JOHN CALVIN REZMERSKI

THE BOOK DREAM

Trying to find a home
for the circus animals –
at the last minute before departure –
hi ho, off to England –
I am reminded I have not found a place
for the camel, the lions, the rhino.
And here they are on my doorstep,
my family unable to feed them,
the man who brought them from the circus
saying it will cost zippity-buzz
to feed this one and zippity-buzz-buzz
more for that. No one is happy.
And there is no way of resolving things.
I call the humane society and they are at a loss.
"You can never get out of them
one tenth of what you put in,"
the man from the circus says.
"No way of getting book value."

Now it is clear. This is a dream.
The too many circus animals
represent my too many books.
Too many, and I can't put them down.
Feeding is reading.
I can't get a reading
on the anteater. I squat down
and stare into its face.
I know I have strange tastes.

PORTRAIT IN ORANGE

The woman in dull purple blouse,
black slacks, purple socks, white shoes,
is trying to peel an orange.
Not much luck.
Nothing orange about her –
she is neither sweet nor sour
and her thumbs are too blunt
to get under the skin.
Smooth-haired she sits,
feet hooked under her chair.
She is deep-eyed thin,
with big hands, and
hunches her shoulders emphatically.
Her hands rip the orange.
Emphatically, she chews,
not free
to enjoy an orange,
but determined to master it.

FREYA MANFRED

WHITE MOTHS

At dusk
thousands of white moths
descended from the trees
and streamed
toward the lake.
They fluttered
inches above the surface
without touching the water
or each other.
Like gigantic snowflakes
in a ground blizzard,
the soft mute moths
danced together
until it was too dark
to see.
So I went to bed
and dreamed
a field
of white flower petals
was carrying a black mountain
into the sky –
and the next morning
they were gone.

WORDS ABOUT DEATH

I have always had words.
But for the moment of death
I have no words.

Even for my father's death,
and how I miss him.
No words.

The only person who might have
something true to say
is the dead man,
who has come back into this bed
with his hands crossed over his chest,
and his mouth closed forever.

Come back from the place he went
when words left us both,
and he followed.

RICHARD LYONS

WAITING

The sudden rain had washed away
the bee's lunch in the white phlox.
Nature betrays, is inconsistent.
The widow in gray went
Weekly to her safety-deposit box.
It contained nothing. "But it may,"
she said, "some day."

The paintings on the new walls
of the old museum turned their backs
on the open mouths of the viewers
standing in ruffled shirts and overalls.
Sunset purples, reds, and blacks
rolled down the pavement into sewers
coloring the underground telephone calls.

I was uncertain which way to go.
Lights were off on the second floors.
There were no open doors
in buses or department stores.
The sign on the traffic lights said No.
The sun that should have been gone
hung on.

A dog slept in the park,
moving its feet in an ideal chase.
Tossing an empty can of beer,
a lady stood as it grew dark

at last and left her place,
glanced at me with a hard face,
muttered, "I'm getting out of here."

I took her place against the bricks
and waited.
The walls were bare or streaked
with ancient ads and politics.
From the buildings slow death leaked,
but I was unintimidated
and used to being in such a fix.

Which was the city and which
was in the unreal air
of my looking inward? It was not
a real question, as the dog
was not real but an illusionary bitch.
But I sat and waited there
in the midst of my imaginary fog
until Walt Whitman on his nightly jog
stopped to say I was in his favorite spot.

DAVE ETTER

BOONDOCKS

Now, if you live in the country
and the farmer next door plants soybeans
right up to your back porch,
well, then you learn to like soybeans.
But this year he plants corn,
and since you've always liked corn
you break out in little snatches of song
as you pad about the 1910 frame house
that creaks like an old ship in the wind.
"What's to be so happy about?"
says the wife, looking for packed suitcases
stacked up near the staircase.
"Oh it's nothing at all," you say.
So she frowns and dusts another table,
and you head for that first iced-cold beer
which tastes so good about 9 A.M.
"It's not like you to sing," she says.
"Boondocks," you say. "Boondocks."

THE YELLOW MAN

Not cowardly,
not afraid to speak out,
and not Chinese,
no,
but yellow skin
the color of old newsprint,
or an aged sunflower
if you happen to catch him
leaning up against
a light pole or picket fence
some afternoon in late autumn.
Yellow hat, too,
and often a mustard shirt
or butter-colored pants.
We call him "Yellow,"
or "The Yellow Man."
He knows it,
he's heard it many times,
yes,
and he knows it's not because
he's scared of fights,
or bullies, or anything.
Yellow, yellow, yellow,
he's always looking like
a yellow teddy bear,
the kind you found
in your childhood attic
on those long winter Sundays.
Look, here he is now,
coming at us,
breaking in a pair
of yellow-bean shoes.

ETHNA McKIERNAN

DEORA DÉ

for my father

We walked through a tunnel of fuschia
and he called the bushes *Deora Dé.*
"From the Irish," he said, *Tears of God.*
How like him it was to pull his other language
from the air like that,

Threading the red blaze of color
and its teardrop song to the sorrow spent
by one creating it, petal by detailed petal
added to a burden of immense particulars
in a world still daily being made.

My father – his thin shoulders angling
through the patched tweed jacket,
our hands linked by the old stories,
fused history cast in common bone.
And the wild fuschia light
on the West Cork mountains
that October afternoon.

THE NEED TO SLEEP

To hide. Be dead
to what disturbs you when awake.
To crawl into God's immense hands,
the lost sheep come home.
To skim the ache off your bones
with pure inertia,
calm the din in your brain
by entering the cave of dreams.
To stop the ferrets gnawing
at the ribs of your soul.
As rejuvenation, the night-food
needed for wrestling down
the giants of the morning.
To meet yourself alone
beyond the worst nightmare
and hold one foot firm,
saying "no," utterly not.
To let go deliberately
and lose the tail of breadcrumbs
Hansel left you, walking
headlong into the forest
holding nothing
that you've ever known.

HUGH FOX

ZEN AND OTHER SIZES

You're disowned!" she (89)
screams and hangs
up
because I discover (at age 59)
that my old "Bohemian"
grandmother (Russ/Roos) was a
Jew,
the same week
my Brazilian wife
finally pushes me into
telling her brother "You
don't have a Green Card,
you have a Master's in
Electrical Engineering,
go get a job in
Brazil already, a year and a
month here is enough,"
and the Academy Awards
flash on
King Gordon
Lish and his court thrive
and little mags get
100 submissions a
month and take 7-10
pieces a year and my
"pieces" are long because
(*War And Peace*) I've
got all these sermons to
volley out at the world,
and Chris says "I don't want to
talk to you tonight," something

wrong in school, some girl
hit him, trying to father at
1500 miles away, like
gloves into a germfree
lab, robo-arms into
radioactivity, the oldest known
Jewish cemetery on the
Mount of Olives, an
old Cantor sounding like
a muezzin,
crack-, sob-, break-ing
through wails of Hebrew
gutteralness,
"Why have I come into this
world, my days are like
water and death like
infinite sand."

CIRCLING

The intensity of the slow
black birds circling toward
the curdled, cauldroned
silent, cold West,
the contours of my brain flowing
with the slow contours of
the clouds, Emily's eyes,
I still haven't looked at her
hands, the warm fur bed
engulfing me, even the pain
in my back pushing back
inevitability.

ISRAEL EXCURSION

Hotel, buses, one of the drivers
had refused to follow the
itinerary and he'd gotten
fired, float in The Dead
Sea, Massadah, a Kibbutz,
"Is there entertainment in
the hotel at night? And
what if you get tired?"
asks his wife. And
Mrs. Lowy is "concerned,
very concerned, with the heat
and the sun."

ARCHIBALD HENDERSON

ACORNS

Acorns are exploding on the sidewalk
and birds have gone into their winter hush.
The clock has begun to slow down again.
One tune thrives on several frequencies.
If it survives the winter, it will glow,
come spring, like an ingot tonged in a furnace.

Precipitous hours and temperatures
juggle the mercury through solstice days
in the carnival Christmastide and beyond.
Brave red faces cluster in dooryards to build
snowmen and throw snowballs (disdaining the blast)
or guide sleds down hillsides and suck icicles.
Underground, thieves are working to rob earth
of its nutriment and send up quick flares
of bloom and foliage after the world turns.
Holiday bowls, emptying trash, will nourish
the soil's aptitude and the genesis
of a complete turnaround in the outlook.

There is a fraudulence to winter cold:
it does not last. The frantic above-ground stir
is more than matched by what goes on beneath.
A little tune beginning with the fall
is about to recapture its momentum.
Suddenly with March, it turns symphonic,
mockingbirds find their voices, burst into song,
a small oak springs up here and there, earth changes,
humans learn to live again among flowers.

CARPENTERS

The man upstairs has turned carpenter.
He is no ordinary person.
He came in with a key I did not know he had.
He has made his noise welcome in that emptiness.
Though I play the concertos of Mozart,
I cannot drown him out.

I do not know what he's doing up there.
I called the lady, who works days;
she says he belongs there: it's proper.

Sudden noises alarm me.
This carpenter's haphazard:
I never know when a blow will strike.
Sometimes he works cajolingly.
Then there's a muffled sound. As from a dark closet.
He should be out by bedtime.
Surely the lady will be back.

Does my music bother him?
I am afraid to go Baroque.
He might explode in a fury of nails.

New thunder! Can it be from outside?
They are building a surprise world.
Is it incompatible with present arrangements?
The carpenter upstairs replies with impatient sounds.
Best I continue the Mozart.

IT ALWAYS HAPPENS

Nothing good's happened in ages
on the planet
on the planet or off

neon still works the bars
girls work the streets
(boys likewise)

men throw their shoulders out
at pro practice
the sudden appearance of a flush in poker
stuns the table
but the cards keep flying

what's with you? she cried
nothing, I said
then why the squeaky voice?
it happens under Leo, I said
it always happens under Leo

8/24/88

THE LOST TABERNACLE

The sledgehammer of the most Holy Writ
echoes but faintly in the fairy stories
and marriage rites that slipped through censors to claim
spots among bloodshed, kick-of-a-mule thunder.
Organ interludes pump life into stained glass
that fronts on risky streets with heavable stones.
There are no poor folk anywhere to be seen.

These are times when the heart's crystal ball clouds
with pity. Knees sink to the floor at odds
with equilibrium. A great bell tolls
unremittingly, and a breeze blows out
offerings of candles to the Most High.
The great vault, like some oxygen tent, secures
breath for a multitude trapped in ecstasies.

The bulbs in the candelabra tremble
and begin to flower so riotously
they spangle the aisle with blossoms in color:
red, black, violet, sepia, fresh rainbow
out of the refractions drawn from the white.
A garden new-made in this tabernacle
welcomes its breakaway tribes of wild hue.

WHEN SHE REFUSED TO BE COMFORTED

It was different when she said it.
She wore a lilting red dress that flared slightly . . . .
She spilled genuine tears down the screaming mascara
of her face – a shriek told her off on the phone:
"Negligence! You're not getting it done!"

Then I threw at her feet the rhinestones of sympathy
and she spurned them. When in doubt let it out. To begin with,
my pulse was perpetual motion. Eyes blinked pain.
"It makes no sense," I told myself. The last I heard,
it made sense, and you better believe it.

At first it was awful. I mean awful. You laugh
some things off, but this was unique. Then I shut up.
I was calm. I knew the next day I would seethe,
keep cool now and enjoy it. Superiority never hurt anyone.
I mean deep-down superiority. But tomorrow, let it blow.

9/29/88

DARA WIER

THE LOST PASTOR

The good pastor had reverted
to her natural hair color.
Out of nowhere a raven in a dog collar
appeared to guide her,
but then along came a red-tailed hawk
who got its messages all mixed up.
She evolved into a mole
and rooted through her congregation's lawns.
She grubbed for a living all summer long.
After she'd checked the sopranist's hair
for lice and the deacon's armpits for nits
she found herself in danger of losing
her entire fold. They were drifting away
like dandruff. She'd seen enough and was stuck
in a rut. She knew she needed a fresh start
or a new hat. She lacked will and Will
had gotten himself entangled with a tramp-
infested mailman on the lam. She practically
had no body. And her hair kept falling out
of what little skull she'd managed to keep,
abandoning ship, mutiny amongst the stowaways,
stowaways thick as lice, bugs burrowing tunnels
in her brain furrows.
Essentially smug, turncoat elders blandly
recommended she go in for early retirement
or at least have herself irradiated.
She considered that, much to the dismay
of her acupuncturist, but gave it up
after pouring diesel fuel over her firemaps

and calculating just how far away she lived
from any port. In a storm of self-decoration
she no longer accepted alms.
She accepted hair nets which she employed
to imprison migrating darning needles.
She fed them on lice she's been fattening
on quarters. A few had grown as large
as barns. She darn well knew she treaded
on very thin ice. But her Great Aunts had
taken pains to drive it into her.
She was no quitter. Any qualms she once embraced
she watched fall through a hole in the ice
where schools of hair-eating fish,
suddenly rich overnight, upset the delicate
balance of their tightly-knit civilization.
They over-built and had too many nests
and were threatened with extinction.
Sadly, their one distinction, an absolute lack
of a sense of direction, abandoned them
in the face of so many choices.
Their one hope rested in the tiny hands
of the town officials, an un-elected snarl
of two-bit scoundrels, who throughout the endless
months of winter never once turned the town fountain off.
It became a salt lick for wounded trucks
and lost caravans of permanently-stained saints.
The lost pastor had grown large and tired
of the fish market man and his wife
and the fireman and the firehouse.
She'd become restless, careless and shiftless,
equivocating, canceling last minute visits
to the sick and dying, failing to report

to funerals and weddings. The formulas
of secret ingredients she'd long-guarded
she no longer needed. They'd be left
to generations of other pastors. Well,
everybody's got a compass needle in a smokestack,
a powderkeg in a tinderbox, a little bit of hearsay,
a headful of gossip, a gimmick, a spit curl,
a demographic, a statistic. It's just good business
to send memorial donations directly to your favorite
charity.

STEVEN TARLOW

SUKKOT

Our wine is from the Finger Lakes;
Its head is beer-thick when chilled.
We have blessing fruit
With its strange neutral taste, the last
Of the summer fruit
And the autumn fruit as it nears
Its fever pitch, brine tomatoes.

To set our teeth on edge, walnuts
And prunes to clear our digestion.
We have honey from bee farms
Near the reservoir, local melons,
Joints of meat and candy apples
For the children whose cheeks

Already freeze in the delicate stems
Of their nostrils. Shivering, I sit
In our sukkah and think of
The Hasid near the Western Wall
Who bent so grotesquely with his lulav.
Flexing bony knees. His feet
Were luminous in their felt slippers

And his calf veins bulged.
They remind me now, of the gnarled orchards
Beside the Finger Lakes, the hum
Of outboard motors cheerful
With erotic promise. Fingering
The engraved vine leaves, I lift

My full cup. My family huddles
Around me and the Ushpizin,
The seven guests, look on
From their doleful wallhanging.
Soon, I hope, they will leave

The corn-stalk, the mountain,
And the dazed ram
By its altar, the harp
Silent on its nail. I drink down
The Finger Lakes wine; it dizzies me
Like a sudden breath

Of outboard motor fuel.
My eyes close and I summon
My seven imaginary guests. I feel their cold
Hands first, covering my eyes.
In my hand they place an etrog
With its erect nipple poking
Through the wool muff.

In childhood once, alone
In the house with a high fever
I stood at the head of the stairs.
I lifted my arms and felt
The weight of molecules
On my palms. I felt their separateness.

Even then my shoulders tingled
And I could not bring my arms down.
Tomorrow, I will join
Etrog and lulav, no matter
How much they strain
To stay apart. I will revolve
My hips and concentrate grotesquely.
I will lay the fruit then

In its virginal canister.
Weeks from now, when
The first snow threatens
I will pry open the lid

And part the desiccated wool.
What is left I will cup like a fossil egg.
I will rub it gently, as a child might
Until its ridges are smoothed down
And its mild smell fills the house.
With palms closed, I will keep it
Warm all winter.

WILLIAM HEYEN

THE WANDERING

(for my wife)

Early August already yellowjacket drones
wander aimlessly over village lawns no

color of blossom attracts them their
seasonal work is done I've

watched them trudge in the sweet juice
of a smashed pear & not sip they're

dying, their brittle winged forms now
sensing dimensions of being prior

to birth in the crystalline patterns of species
by which their queen still survives who

will need them again from the beginning,
& this isn't it is God itself as

over time we'll need to take leave let
go soon ourselves maybe a decade or three

& then our dying from this home
where our children – our daughter married

just yesterday – grew, & then this wandering
into the aisles of our childhood orchards past

woods & ponds & crows in distances of dream
& remembrance, stayed by nothing

as I walked from the back of the church
toward you & her husband-to-be,

flaring out there finally the same
creation our daughter turning to me & trying

not to cry, she in her satin gown, carrying
roses, & we to be born from her again.

WAS

Parts of the road were piled up in a field.
In thousands of lengths of asphalt, you could see
white or yellow stripes, & those umber cats' eyes,
& fenders fendering out from this conglomerate,
batteries & seatsprings, shreds of tire, aerials

twisted into question marks. Where the road
once was was now no thing,
not even trench. Pure nothing. You could see
clear through the planet to stars winking,
so you reached in, & your hands disappeared,

so you gave one foot, then the other, then
one shoulder, then your conscious head . . . .
What remains: this field of road-rubble
beside where the road has been,
but meadow entities begin, don't they,

poking up in it, goldenrod among the engine blocks,
mice chasing crickets through tailpipes & hoses.
You've got the feeling the road's crumbling.
The wind's blowing up through where our traffic was,
whatever the hell it was, & you're listening.

MOLE

This many years later, a mole
tunnels into a mass grave,
only a few inches below surface,
but, yes, a grave.

The mole enters a ribcage,
progresses past a skull,
scrapes its claws
on desiccated bones.

The mole, it goes without saying,
utters its ignorant light
in that dark, raises mounds
in cursive across the grave,

searching for what? Bulbs
of wild onion, roots
of erika. That mammal's
urgency of being, its

penmanship: "*Nach Auschwitz,*
ein gedict zu schreiben
ist barbarisch." The soul
of language: raised tunnels.

MELANIE RICHARDS

WILD SWANS

We imagine them in repose,
long necks tilted back
as they hesitate, then swoon

over the black sheen
of the pool, small clouds
of contemplation, and yet

when the world shakes
and glints and beckons,
they rise over the green

yearning branches
of the cypress, all sweep
and ache and glide,

out of the despair
of the unfathomable waters
in a line aimed straight

for the eye of god.

NOCTURNE

By day I rise and shed the weight
that rides me in the night: doubt
seethes in the sleepless dark,
haggard bird, preening and weeping.

RICHARD CARR

JONES'S WOODS

Awake and dressed – no need for an alarm,
although it's early and the sky is black –
I grab my twelve-gauge shotgun from the rack
and set out after ducks by Jones's farm.
But as I near his pond, the woods disarm
my eagerness: a clatter farther back,
just clicks and scrapes of twigs that seem to track
my footsteps through the brush – as if some harm
could come of it. Unless, great God, it's Jones.
I stop. I load a shell. There's not a sound.
In dawn's gray light, the treetops faintly sway,
an open grave of tangled insect bones.
An owl swoops, snatches something from the ground.
Old Jones, his woods, I know the tricks they play.

ROLAND FLINT

WILLIAM STAFFORD'S LAST DAY

Up early to jog and write, alert
For what might show – such as
An Apache word for love, new dirt
On the mole, a snowy pass.

So careful and youthfully fit,
We said he's a cinch for ninety.
He'd have been amused by that,
Knowing: any time is plenty.

His poem was done, when Dorothy
Called and he went to help her. So,
If too soon for us, it was a worthy
Moment for his heart to go.
For whatever epic after that,
He was readier than we, no doubt.

WHEN I INVENTED THE ROSE

It was a kind called red,
because then I knew
only blood-velvets
kissing open like silk,
without a tulip's punning.

Just the licky tip inside,
scents of musk, vanilla,
lavender loams of Kazanluk,
and so subtle you must
put your face in it.

Velvet for the petals,
as I say, or angora.
Thorns? – left by such
an avid tonguing but
not in the design.

THE ETRUSCANS

1. *At The Etruscan Well In Perugia*

Three or four hundred years before
Christ, the Etruscans dug a hole
at the best confluence of springs,
here in Perugia, and built a well
to last, if not forever, till now:
the centuries have piled on 450
meters or so of the layered busyness
since, so you have to walk down
many steps through an excavation
in order to see its top, under which
are the great central travertine
beams weighing 80 tons apiece
leaning to pinch in place, if
not forever, the central stone, far
above the unstill waters, circled,
up to the beams, by the great walls
of brick-like rock, down which
constantly trickle the abiding
ingenuities of Etruscan water.

2. *At The Etruscan Museum In Rome*

Besides wells, architecture, and
engineering to move a quarry,
they seem to have been best at
killing, necrotic art, and sex
as you'd expect from its sound,
elegant, cruel, deft and smart,
Etruscan. Rectitude, knife-rasp,
forced entry, Etruscan. Arms
long as Giacometti, horse-clop,
empire, deep wells, big stones,
javelins, carriages, Etruscan.
Males, carnage, sex and death.
Power to move love and terrify.

FLOWER

The crude little rose must be
aluminum, it is so light
it could be made of rice
or Rice Krispies, gun gray,
a fully opened blossom
of the rose you found
along the street and picked
up. Now it blooms from the center
of an International Rotary wheel
you got for bringing poems to men
whose business is to aluminize
anything – even a rose: which is,
sort of, what you did right back,
for a fat fee, at the Rotary lunch,
bootlegging poetry in by limerick,
from innocent suggestives to
the bawdily ambiguous to
a fully aluminized rose.

JEAN VALENTINE

LONG IRISH SUMMER DAY

A lorry scatters
hay down the road
red as blood.

Down by Tommy Flynn's
a young man is sowing
in the ten o'clock sunset

sowing salt tears on the road
– not for the ice, we already have sand.

Sun and moon shine into our glass room,
two countries, two cities,
two glass houses:
a shotgun is hanging on the wall.

DONALD JUNKINS

THE WHITE GOAT IN THE LIGHT RAIN, XIAMEN

Here above the temple, I see
harbor ships coming and leaving, day
by day. They blow great horns,
on the move. One ship stays.
All through rainy

season, the anchor lights go on
at dusk, glow through the night.
One day in April, I study
the ship closer from a crowded shore.
No one in sight.

The anchor chain is algae
green, the water line is rust.
At the bottom of my mountain, rain
begins, deepens the darkening green.
Monstrous boulders hover in the high mist.

Once I stood on one at dawn,
looking beyond the harbor toward Taiwan,
the elephant back smooth as a tomb.
Now this white goat up there in the rain
standing as if unseen.

RAINY SEASON, XIAMEN

The white butterfly between me
and the top of my ninety-nine stairs
jump-starts the heavy air
of afternoon. I can see

three ships in the spring
mist, crickets sleeping
through meadow dew, antennae
anchored in old Amoy.

White peony petal, flitting
out of my nap dream, gone
into the green fur peaches. It
returns and goes clean, as bone.

MOUNTAIN MIST, XIAMEN

Rowers on the campus lake
take turns drifting,
bird boats contemplate
the fisherwoman lifting

her empty net, beating the far shore
with a bamboo pole.
The rowers imitate each other's
leisure. Later, her net is full.

GLENNA LUSCHEI

PRINCIPAL

I didn't get along with
my high-school principal –
She must have known
behind her back I called her
Gravel Gertie.

She accused me of the cardinal
sin – bad planning.
I wonder what I learned from her
ruler, groundings, notes to home?
I still plan
badly.
Only the deadline gets me going. Excuses, excuses. Just one more day
which I will waste
dashing from beauty to beauty.

You'd think I'd learn.
At graduation
when she assigned me to pick
lilies of the valley for the podium
I had to cross her.
I said, "Give me a committee."
Always cross authority,
that's me. Fight with every motorcycle cop.

My father's words:
take your punishment and go on
but I've lived long enough to know
I provoke the firing squad.

Mata Hari had her reasons
for passing secrets to the enemy.
Danger ups the ante.
Visions of the guillotine
smuggle out the soldier.

Gravel Gertie got me going. You remember
her from Little Abner.
Snow-white hair and goiter at the throat.
Never drank the kick-a-poo joy juice
the rest of us lived on.
That I still thrive on.

Gravel Gertie got me
early.
"I live by the runes not the rules,"
I told my boss the last time
I got fired.
Somehow I get by
dashing from beauty to beauty.

PINE CONES

Wtih little pain you bear a daughter.
A golden child who loves you
as much as you love her.
She places her golden head in your lap.
She swings from the pine in a cut-out tire:
all of it meant to be.

They tell you the gods are jealous.
You ask, "Jealous of goodness?"
Once the doctor cut a half moon
in her eardrum.

More children arrive as pine cones.
You hold them on your lap, prickles or no.
The gods are fuming.
But isn't it meant to be?

Your friends write her life
had meaning. Life was golden.
You see her descend the golden staircase.
The disease attacked her DNA.

The people die in this plague
like flies in the eyes of African children.
She lies in her wedding dress
beneath a pine. Too horrible to understand.
This was meant to be.

KEVIN BEZNER

CROWS IN PINES

I hear them
call as they
fly over

the house to
the pines out
back. As they

land, only a
faint puff of
snow from

branches,
nothing more
perfect than these

twelve crows in
this bank of
trees.

EAMON GRENNAN

WEATHER

After three or four days of persistent rain
something like panic sets in, a sense
of being smothered by wet noise,
nowhere to turn and nothing to be done
but hang on, hold out until some fresh
thing happens. I think of middle age like this,
when you can see bleakness set in
and no change, farther outlook only
more of the same, and you find yourself
saying this is the way things have to be
for good now. Even those you love
get stranger and stranger: you grow
more fragile with each other, thinking
of warm things in their burrows who
listen to the wind's loud mouth at the door –
how it bites and gouges all above ground.

But then the weather settles abruptly,
sudden as a reprieve, and that's the way
you start to see your life – as if you'd
been let off again and not discovered
wanting. In the suddenly auspicious
light-broken breezes out of the southeast
the sturdy panels of a well-made shirt,
white cotton drying on the line, seems
a hopeful canvas on which, between
now and evening time, anything
can happen – wind filling the shirt-sail
with a taste for adventure – and even

after eleven at night you can see
the pair of swans on the lake are two
incandescent glimmers of possibility
under a fitful moon, and the last
blackbird won't give in to the dark
but goes on, invisible as he is, singing
until your daughter wakes and says
Dad, I can hear the bird, it's laughing.
Is the rain all gone? and before
you can tell her how things are, she is
asleep again and the house is spinning
its own sure silence round your lives.

MICHAEL MOOS

BLOODROOT

This is where the fire swept through the trees like a blinding hand,
devouring the small plants and the nests,
climbing up the trunks of great trees while I slept miles away,
taking it all into the air and disappearing with the stars.
This is where I could not walk any further one day,
where I stood still and saw nothing but charred ground and ash,
where a wind rose up in my chest and died,
where I could not remember my name and lost my hands,
where my breath moved like a dead fish floating down the muddy river,
where my words and sentences abandoned me like old lovers.
This is where I come back a year later and see
the single bloodroot flower rising, white, fragile, clear,
opening its eight translucent petals shaped like silent tongues.
This is where I stand before the fire at its center,
look into it for what seems years, let it come into every part of me,
let it burn clean the forest inside my body,
taking away all the fear and the doubt and the dark memories.
This is how I let its quiet roots reach down into the current of my blood
as long as I can take it, before I have to turn away.

TRACKS IN THE MUD

I wanted the words to come down out of my arm
like a herd of antelope leaping in the tall grass and the light,
black horns shining and opening small invisible wounds in
  the wind.
I wanted to feel the darkness between the stars come down
to breathe against the window where I sleep.
I wanted an old truth from the dust and the fossils
and the cries of tundra swans high above the silent houses,
my heart making its sound of slow mud . . . .
I could not recall the sound of her voice in the branches of
  the winter trees.
I could smell the clear water running in the distance,
the delicate rain beginning far off in the hills.
I was in need of sleep, the little death that comes to us.
I was tired and beaten and afraid to close my eyes.
In my sinking, there were faces and birds above an ocean . . . .

MAYFLIES

I talked with her in a lovely old city garden last night.
Not a slender hand reaching out of memory, but an ordinary human being
come back to turn over the rough stones one more time.
I thought the flowering vines and the falling light would protect us . . . .
But this morning I hear something in my voice
that has not been there before, something outside of hope and loss.
The closest I can come to it is the moment the long grass
shows its underside, that lovely brown color of earth and quiet death.
I see it, too, at the farthest edge of the daisies' drying petals,
or in the silver wake left behind by a simple boat,
fanning out and slowly disappearing like a mayfly's wing.
Remember how we used to take them from the cabin's dark screens,
between our fingers, and let them go in the August air?

SECRET WORK

Soon this light will be gone and the trees will continue their secret work in the dark.
The small white stone lying in the tall grass will resemble the moon
you have always wanted to pull into yourself.
A bird will call from the bare branches, and you will know it is time to go.

WILLIAM HATHAWAY

WEDDING SONNET FOR HER

Stupid Robin, hunched ragged in icy wind,
believes he's the first bird arrived who sounds
bold trills to bring back golden green, to bend
down apple-blossomed boughs in snowy mounds.

Blithe bird! Doesn't he know his cunning fellows
never left, but gorged at a spilling seed trough
all winter long – because a hole to heaven billows
a new age tropic with choice and gracious sloth?

Brave bird! He knows and doesn't think he's dumb
to sing in triumph of his flight. He knows
a gift of springing seed and to where he's come
by where he goes, that only living water flows.

Wise Robin's chosen true. Today let his song
be ours: in Loving, Love sings forever strong.

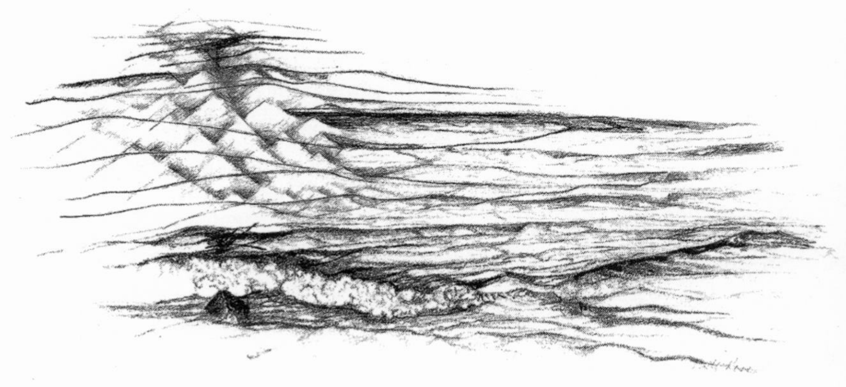

RAIN

By James Ashe

Sometimes he would go out in the evening. At other times, he would stay inside. It did not seem to make much difference. He could not understand how he had ended up like this. Was he born for it? In the morning before he got out of bed, he would lie awake and watch the rain spread against the window. The rain was colorless, with a certain weight making a sound as it hit the window. It changed everything to wetness. The grass, the window sill, the door were all different at least for a while. It even changed aspects of these surroundings that experience had taught him should remain relatively constant. The inlet of water visible from the door disappeared, the nearest peak toppled, the road became shorter. One day last week, the haze was tinged with pink and looked as if the land were being drenched with blood. Except for the rain, his life now knew little change.

It was difficult to keep track of time. He had definite memories, some distinct and vivid, but he could not assign them to a place in his past. Rather, he could not assign them to a particular place or time. That day in that place could have been before or after another day in another place. Both days were somewhere in the past, he was fairly sure. Were the people he remembered real? He probably did meet them at some time, but had not seen them for years. Perhaps they were dead now.

He had been living in that place for some time, several years he thought. He had arrived with a sense of optimism, or something like it. He had known the place before as a child. The road weaved down the valley to the small inlet where the sea had insinuated itself. The inlet was shallow, there was a mountain, beyond that the ocean. He had considered a different place, one where he could view the sea directly but had decided against it in the end. The sight of the open sea shocked him at times. He had been able to cope with its bigness and violence, but now he preferred to look at it sideways out of the corner of his eye.

Yesterday he met a man on the road that went past his house and down to the sea. They talked about the weather. He was certain he had had the same or a similar conversation before. Fine day, thank God. Yes, good for the time of year. It looks as if there may be a change. He had noticed that such discussions were mirrors to the mind. Merely a probe into one's mental processes; the weather was only the tool.

He had difficulty with prediction. It did not apply to everything. He was able to place his feet to avoid dips in the uneven surface of the road. He could catch a jar falling from a shelf before it hit the stone floor. Although little changed, each moment he was different. The person who ate breakfast no longer existed at midday, and yet another wandered around the house by nightfall. When he was younger, he had thought, and perhaps it was true, that the passage of such short amounts of time made little difference. This had been a form of comfort to him. Now he relied on nothing. Past experience accounted for little. He knew that tomorrow somehow would be different.

SAUDAMINI SIEGRIST

CLOUD

You've been on mountaintops
when the weather descends
and you lose yourself in a cloud.
The cloud that surrounds you
on the mountain is torn
like a mist, like God's breath,
like the terror you feel.
You can't tell how close
is the cliff or how high
or if the ground underneath you
is really rock. At times,
in the mountains, the atmosphere
you breathe can shock you
out of your self. You hear
sound through a powerful wind
tunnel that opens into the sky.

Ancient writings tell how,
in days long ago, the human
being could fly.
Not the flight you imagine,
not physical flight,
but a captivation of the breath,
an inner rapture that tears
you from your body.

GLASS JAR

If you allow me to console you, I will
collect in a glass jar fragrances
of jasmine and cardamom, the pinkest petal,
the faintest blush, a campfire flame that dances

all night like a cobra entranced, the shimmer
in air of an oasis, a singed moth.
I'll capture the moon's reflection in a mirror
of sky inside the jar, a monk's breath,

all my earthly treasures I will place
there, a see-through tear, the sloughed off
chrysalis of my life. I'll keep a trace
in the morning of our meeting with enough

time for dreams you dream to come true.
You can smash the jar if you want to.

WHY I PREFER WATERCOLOR

Because it is applied in a wash,
because the tint of fire in watercolor flickers,
because watercolor mirrors a grey eye,
because color is mixed in puddles on a palette,
because the strength of watercolor is in dilution,
because color is its only contour,
because it blurs churches,
because the French Riviera has an orange outline of
  watercolor,
because watercolor dries more radiant, more faint,
because bamboo brushes of horse hair bristle are its
tools,
because it obeys the laws of chemistry for play,
because lobster boats of watercolor float on an ocean
  of raw umber,
because you can't crop watercolor,
because the shadows of watercolor are really lavender,
because fog is its subject,
because of its frequent rain,
because it moves in waves of color across spokes of light.

CLARK COOLIDGE

STRODE ROAD

Woody, do you stand there like a pump
addressing vim to all the golden vistas
lashing yourself for the stripes on your shirtfront?

I never saw you the least divided
mere shadow of a silly caper on the square
you fought out, lasted, elbowed in
the loneness of all race

Nothing could cow you
you bone up wherever the flats go dry
take a loose teaspoon and turn your head
and turn your head

They're lying to you behind the rimrock of plan
pianos in harm you stove in their hat racks
come back into areas thrumming with grin
on your hat there is topspin

And the drops at the final stall
there you were stoned Chinese
when the wires wore out and home dimmed
you dome of a seatless calm
stone appender plain
shock still of the learning of a man

4XII94

THE ELABORATE HALLWAY

Cylindrical ballad
that shows barnyard tendencies
we have copied your wristlike scatter
on a broad pavement to Ohio
and equally melded imbroglio
the lights were off

A contained botany
Newton me hearties
he pinned it up down on stage
in a veering message down the side
haul off and light me
I have been barely available
and I meet the mustard

Was wearing an insectlike vest
invented in whole fire flavors
product ranch?
come back to the western holder for things
capsule placer, lancer enclosed
we three were the walls
there was no ceiling

Apres gig
the waltz thought
steered into our place
tune a house for that lemon lightbulb
a rubber clock through which
you can see the baseball tremble

Lollobrigida Plantagenet
I rest Hydrox from the Plain of Standbys
a lucky locker of things prehensile
good beyond trouble to truth
did you trouble to reach?

X94

ODE TO SADE
Sade, going up a rope of your own sapping case
someone has taken care to turn your cheek to cheeses
hahaha, they scream at you
and come down with something untied
the cattle version of human woes
is this the violet portion of the world?
stiff on it!
a shambles of a nation's ladders
never come to rest
(you never took a hike)
all this a business in the unblinking
from which the head is still missing

4XII94

CHARLOTTE OTTEN

CALIFORNIA MAY

I can't get northern California
seasons straight. It's May. The grasses
have already browned. In Michigan

(my state) they're just beginning
to turn green. Those leaves and berries
clasping Highway 1 – those can't be blackberries

ripening in May? At home they've barely
leafed. It takes hot August and September
to make them black. Air exhales leaping shapes:

Queen Anne's lace, yellow hawkweed,
purple phlox, lilies, stippled robins,
ocean ripe for surfing, strawberries

big as apples. The thaw began at home
a week ago. Robins in egg. Strawberries are dreams
of June that fit the mouth.

CLARENCE MAJOR

STILLNESS AND VERTIGO

I enter.
What is that chanting?
Here
among vestments
and melons
bowls and brine kegs
filled
and crossbars of silver,
gilded bronze, velvet –
where dancing is done
in trick-mirrors
where one self
runs the risk of being lost
in the fibrous tissues
and fantasies of another,
you enter.
My entrance meets
yours on the turning floor.
We touch in the mirror,
crazed with fear
of the loss of balance,
like two sacrificial victims
waiting to be beheaded
and left to dry
in ceremonial sunlight,
as a concoction
like wormwood.

CONUNDRUM

In my native language
which is not mine
my name means Always Going.
It is spoken as a request.
In some
recent variant trans-
lations translators have
gotten it wrong
or better still,
stretched its possibilities.
Those that come
to mind say: Going Always
means I request
eye-witnesses at my death.
Going Farther Away means
I request
the inward gaze
of enlightenment
with my worldliness.
Going This Way
means you request
my presence to give
meaning to the lives
we both are trying
to live.

HISTORY AND RENAISSANCE: MARVIN BELL

A Marvin Bell Reader, selected poetry and prose, by Marvin Bell (Middlebury College Press, University Press of New England, Hanover and London, 1994, 232 pp.: $40, cloth; $16.95, paper).
The Book of the Dead Man, poems by Marvin Bell (Copper Canyon Press, Box 271, Port Townsend, WA, 98368, 1994, 80 pp.: $22, cloth; $12, paper).

Someone has come to enchant Marvin Bell. It is an enchantment that has caused a renaissance in the poet as he rises to the occasion of enchantment to create a collection of poems for his enchanting figure to inhabit. We are lucky to bear witness to Marvin Bell's continuing renaissance in *The Book of the Dead Man*. We are equally lucky to have *A Marvin Bell Reader* with which to read a selected history of one man's talent that has helped make American poetry the superb cultural banquet that it is.

The Book of the Dead Man introduces us to Bell's Odysseus. The dead man is the continuous traveler whose body cannot stop thinking about the world that constantly engages him into action. "Drawn by stones, by earth, by things that have been in the fire" ("What Became What: An Autobiography"), Bell's dead man allows him the ideality of the never-ending poem. The symbiosis between beauty and truth is extended into the end of the dead man who joins the Keatsian figures as yet another "foster-child of silence and slow time." Yet Bell awakens his "silent form" out of art and into earth where he becomes nature's thinking. Bell is known for his metaphysical engagement with nature. The dead man poems, of which there is a brief sampler at the end of *A Reader*, allow him to conjoin nature and human nature into the symbiotic relationship between truth and beauty. Each defines the other. Each increases the power of the other.

A Reader reminds us again and again that truth is Bell's icon. His "desire to tell the truth" ("Pages #2"), creates a sensual epistemology that resonates from the words he chooses. What is true is the continuous estrangement of body from mind. Stepping into estrangement is the stranger:

As simply as a self-effacing bar of soap
escaping by indiscernible degrees in the wash water
is how a man may change
and still hour by hour continue in his job.
("A Man May Change")

The appearance of the stranger is the appearance of Bell's muse, because it is this appearance that turns the dailiness of living into the ecstatic moments of poetry:

> The day the birds were lifted from my shoulders,
> the whole sky was blue, a long-imagined effect
> had taken hold, and a small passenger plane
> was beating the earth with its wings
> as it swung over the bean fields toward home.
>
> ("The Nest")

In Bell's recounting, "That was life," although "After that, I was another person." Who writes his poems is this "another" who "lives and dies before anyone can find out" ("A Man May Change"). When Bell finds the dead man, he will find the man to whose shoulders the birds have flown.

The man with the birds on his shoulders is the ecstatic poet. "Explode now," he writes in "Ecstasy." He wants "to have opened to the delirium" to follow passion's "Up-welling of forces, serums and fevers," until he is blown apart in the arms of life. His writings look for the heartbeats that drum the world against the faces of his poems.

> The question of what I am up to. I am carving my own face. I am taking responsibility for the furrows on the hillsides and the wheel marks in the grass. I am absorbing all the moisture of a northwest seaside winter. I am closing the walls of my feelings about the deep, insistent winds that ride the bluff. I am in the distance and at home, hurrying to move and hurrying not to move.
>
> ("Pages #2")

Bell feels the insistence of wildness as much as he feels the necessity of home. Such passionate dichotomy gives him only contradiction, and it is contradiction that works to create his poetic. In any situation, Bell does both. He changes and remains "constant." The poet implodes the sentence upon the line by using the phrase. He confronts images with nouns that reveal secrets rather than objects. The way we know the body is through nouns. The body is a noun. It is the noun that will find the dead man:

Ungainly yet mild perhaps,
taking the place of no field,
offering neither to stand in the place of a tree
nor where the water was,
neither under your heel nor floating,
just gradually appearing,
gainless and insubstantial,
near you as always,
asking you to dance.
("The Poem")

Nonetheless, while the extraordinary wildness of secrets is found by nouns, Bell's poems also engage the necessary, ordinary moments of home. He sees these moments as victorious surprises that give us rooms in which we can engage in continuance. In the continuing Zen of "Pages," he writes:

What we do today is hard-won though it be only the drinking of a cup of tea by the window and a steady look at the light in the trees. What we do today will be daring though it be the slow walk of an errand. What we do today will be new though it happen on a local street.

("Pages #3")

It is Bell's "steady look" that allows him to see the dead man in the domesticated, yet storm-tossed, milieu of the grave. We see it coming when Bell is surprised not by joy, but by a sense of "peace in her arms when he did not intend to be (peaceful)" ("Victim of Himself"), because he had been seeing "a long way off the ocean / cresting and falling" and seeing the "Earth up to the stars." He wants to feel the pull of these "passionate tides." He wants to be "a citizen of mud and ash" as the dead man will be, but instead he is safe and feeling "a sense of loss." Ironically, the dead man will lose this sense of loss, linked to the earth as he is, and he will feel every tug and bray of the planet as a confession of his existence:

The dead man is an amphitheater of dramatic performances,
ethereal scripts now written in the air like used radio
signals in space.

The dead man mistakes natural disasters for applause –
erosion in Carolina, quakes in California.
The dead man's shoes are muddy from being constantly
on stage.
("Second Postscript: More About the Dead Man")

Here we have the ultimate, never-ending romantic that Bell cannot be, because as steady as he looks, the earth appears still as dilution, as evaporation.

Bell's "steady look" that is his passionate engagement with earth, is a look that demands the lack of interruption that solitude provides. "Solitude is a small necessary business of the soul" ("Pages #2") where all that matters happens. It is here that Bell carves his "own face" and notes that "Writing is a form of talking to oneself" ("Author's Preface" to the *Reader).* It is here that the many forms of thought nestle in his arms. One of the reasons that we read Bell is to hear him talk about the writing to which he has given his life:

> Another silent period broken. White glue. The time in between stretches of writing takes many forms. An anthology of one-line poems. Titles without lines. Phrases of light that go out for lack of a connection. A sky that celebrates the anniversary of a previous sky. A valveless brass instrument on which one may sound no more than the fragmentary call of a single bugle. Although I suffer writing blocks, I do not believe in them. No, blocked writing is not this loss of language. I suffer *value* blocks. I write to undo or evade the specious and to find the forms for values. Thus, my "writing blocks" are places where the path goes under the brush, where my thinking dead-ends for a while. I have run out of form, or I have run out of values: the consequences are the same.
>
> ("Pages #3")

In solitude, then, is both home and exile. We stay there without sadness when "the poem (is) too long to finish." ("Ten Thousand Questions Answered")

The life of the dead man is also too long to finish. He is a figure busy in the ground. He is a bebopping, never-ending, songs of himself, catacombed creature of science and art. Bell confronts the idea that "Our language stops at the thought of death" ("Pages #2") and extends the reach of

Keats' "Bold Lover" ("Ode to a Grecian Urn") until he can kiss, because whatever "he saw, heard, felt, tasted or smelled, every wave and breeze has its metabolic equivalent in his dreams" ("Second Postscript: More About the Dead Man"). The dead man is impossible. He is Darwinian Zen: "The dead man is absolutely animal" ("About the Dead Man's Not Sleeping"). "The dead man is Darwin's resolution, an ultimate promise" ("About the Dead Man and a Parallel Universe") that the body makes to the mind. Having undergone "metaphysical surgery" ("About the Dead Man and Sin"), the brain loses its mind and becomes the body. But the body is full of itself and has immense power:

> The dead man transcends gravity, clinging to the bottom of the earth, then to the top, first one side then another, impervious to the siren call of those frigid planets which patrol the heavens seeking the victims of black holes.
>
> ("About the Dead Man and Medicinal Purposes")

Vulnerable to the twitches of earth, he becomes whatever this planet does. Amazingly, he is able to make choices. He "swells with metabolic anticipation" ("About the Dead Man's Happiness") as he weighs the impact of life. He always knows what he is doing. He "can spend fifteen minutes opening and closing an umbrella, what a contraption!, its cone changes to a triangle and then a parabola, reordering geometry." He knows all there is to know. He refutes confusion. He does it all. Yet even after overindulgence and "In pain, the dead man puts repetitive phrases to an endless melody, he tries gum and mints, he coats his stomach with pink oxides" ("More About the Dead Man and Medicinal Purposes"), he deals in solutions. He is the master of cause and effect whose "remedy is to hold still" while being moved. What is extraordinary about the dead man is that he is, most eternally, someone to be: a role model, a hero, the center of activity.

It is interesting work getting to know someone well who is dead as dead, who is only alive as dead, only dead as alive. An obverse biography of a life fully engaged in nature lets us watch the words happen as weighted objects that pull us down into the whole idea of the thing. Bell's language is fraught with irony while he studies his own future and makes a good meal of death. Bell places all the objects and ideas that matter against matter itself. Such metaphysical enjambment has the dead man rattling his keys – he is going places – while Bell stands at the hardware store looking at the fallible closure of locks. Bell's poetics of now looking at nothing gives us nothing being itself in the ethos of the dead man. Bell gives us the power implicit in the art that death makes possible:

> The dead man has poetry in his stomach, bowels and genitals.
> In the dead man's inner organs, poems are born, mate, change and die.
>
> ("About the Dead Man and His Poetry")

Which is why "The dead man, like Keats, shall live among the English poets." The dead man is where he belongs.

It is the dead man, then, that brings the birds back to Marvin Bell. What killed him in "The Nest," the birds lifted off his shoulders, is brought back to him by the dead man, whose name becomes a chant for "the nightingale of tradition" and "the masses of sparrows." Birds are flight, are breath, are sin. We follow them to the edge where "A large bird is a universe, an entirety held from above." Such "an entirety" comes at us the way a sentence comes to a line, erasing the boundaries between form and thought, between the physical and the metaphysical. The dead man notes the cessation of boundary. Because "The dead man's brain has undergone metaphysical surgery" ("About the Dead Man and Sin"), he "erases the word for God to better understand divinity." Then:

> When nothing interferes, nothing interrupts, nothing sustains or concludes, then there's no need to separate doing from not-doing or to distribute the frequencies of the thunder into cause and effect.
>
> ("About the Dead Man and Thunder")

All this, because "The dead man speaks God's language." God's language comes from the direct perception of nature while it eats us alive. Word and bird are both "open doors," physical accounts of naming that lead us to "the looping lift and fall of love" within writing.

The dead man appears to be madly in love. Both domestic and wild love themes continue to permeate the writings of Marvin Bell. Such communion creates community. The dead man is in a state of constant knowing because he is never out of touch with the world. He is present to its every rub. He is writing all the texts and reading all the texts simultaneously. As a perfect lover, a perfect reader and a perfect writer, he had been "thought to be disintegrating, dissolving and deconstructing" what Bell calls "the conscience of the planet," but rather he "has been materializing, coalescing and under-structuring." The dead man holds the earth to its task of being the earth, and therefore allows it to become the source of his metaphysics: "Without the dead man, the sunflower would not proclaim its common face, nor the lily sway into biblical cover." ("About the Dead Man and Nature")

The dead man is constantly, and most generously, engaging in creation. He is nature and art; he is the reconciliation of body and mind. "The dead man knows the syntax of rivers and rocks, the one a long ever-qualifying sentence for which no last words suffice, the other the briefest and most steadfast exercise in exclusion." ("About the Dead Man's Speech") Bell has created a figure who thinks with his gut, a figure who enlarges the definition of what it means to think. The dead man is the earth thinking about the earth. On the route from the physical to the metaphysical, he races to the top:

> The dead man's nerves will not give up, his tongue refuses to quit, his brain saves up until it sparks, his blood abandons his extremities to go where needed, his pulse suddenly races, even his eyes lean out to feel before they see.
>
> ("About the Dead Man and *The Book of the Dead Man*")

That "the dead man is a postscript to closure" ("More About the Dead Man and *The Book of the Dead Man*") returns us to the ideality of letting "the poem be too long to finish." The dead man is closure's muse. In *A Reader*, we see Bell searching the journey for the dead man. *The Book of the Dead Man* begins the continuing saga of a new Odysseus who has pulled Bell into the "unheard" whose "soft pipes, play on." Marvin Bell lets us see it coming, this dead man, this intoxicating reversal of ecstasy:

> An intoxicating idea at a distance: to keep something beyond its time is somehow to have kept it forever. No way now to throw it out. The shrunken, fermented apple is not a version of the apple it was. It is another thing, to another purpose.
>
> ("Pages #1")

Not everyone can raise the dead man, but Marvin Bell can and has.

CAROL ELLIS

EDEN, GOATS, ROME, AND VOICES OF LONG AGO

Imperfect Thirst, poems by Galway Kinnell (Houghton Mifflin, Boston and New York, 1994, 81 pp.; $19.95, hardback).
String Light, poems by C.D. Wright (The University of Georgia Press, Athens and London, 1995, 62 pp.; $8.95, paper).
when new time folds up, poems by Kathleen Fraser. (Chax Press, Box 19178, Minneapolis, MN, 1993, 86 pp.; $11, paper).
The Country I Remember, poems by David Mason. (Story Line Press, Three Oaks Farm, Brownsville, OR 97327, 77 pp., 1996; $12, paper).

Galway Kinnell's twelfth collection of poems, *Imperfect Thirst,* opens with a credo or manifesto entitled "The Pen" – about a pen but also about poetry:

> Its work is memory
> It engraves sounds into paper and fills them with pounded
> nutgall.

Ink can be made from the gall nuts of an oak tree. It is a strong image. Poetry for Kinnell is a tough, oak-like business but it is not simply materialistic:

> Under increased concentration the pen spreads its rib, thickening
> the words that attempt to speak the unspeakable.
> These are the fallen angel words.
> Ink is their ichor.
> They have a mineral glint, given by clarity of knowing, even in
> hell.

"Ichor" is the ethereal fluid that took the place of blood in the Greek gods. It is also the discharge from an ulcer. I suspect Kinnell wishes to refer to both, heaven and hell. He does not use words loosely, especially medical words. For him words are a kind of action or behavior and we feel the pressure of his moral involvement in the selection of words, whether in the autobiographical narratives that open this volume or the elegy on his dying sister that closes it. So when he writes a long poem with the title "Holy Shit" that chronicles the authorities on defecating from Plato to Whitman, we refrain from grinning or making silly jokes. We sit up straight and pay attention – or rather, as the poet enjoins us:

> Let us sit bent forward slightly, and be opened a moment
> as earth's holy matter passes through us.

Our physicality is holy, baroque and sometimes apocalyptic. In "The Cellist," Kinnell writes amazingly of the source of the music and the female cellist's body:

> The music seems to rise from the crater left
> when heaven was torn up and taken out of the earth;
> more likely it comes up through her priest's dress,
> up from beneath that clump of hair which by now
> may be so wet with its waters, miraculous as the waters
> the fish multiplied in at Galilee, that
> each strand wicks a portion all the way out
> to its tip and fattens a droplet on the bush
> of half notes now glittering in that dark . . . .

The puritan sensibility, a grandeur of the flesh, is the theme of the erotic poem – "The Night – where the man lies cuddling the woman in bed: "Him like the big folded wings of her" so that "his penis settles along the groove between her buttocks." We are not surprised by the final Miltonic line: "They have been lying on this bed since before the earth began."

Kinnell is an important, perhaps a major, American poet with an impressive range of subjects from hummingbirds to the "ether the Newtonian physicists manufactured / to make good the vacuums in the universe." He covers homely anecdotes, domestic life and academic lectures ("The Deconstruction of Emily Dickinson") in a range of forms, including a series of Persian ghazals. Above and encompassing all, he writes of nature that is both ecological and human, ranging through outer space and our own intestines. In a Wordsworthian meditation on youth and dying ("The Striped Snake and the Goldfinch"), he identifies, as he has in previous volumes, with the snake: "Meanwhile the snake / may have crawled up my spine to sit in my youth / and utter an unsteady flame."

He reminds us of Eden and our traditional myths. His pen is an old-fashioned fountain pen, not a ballpoint and "like the camel at an oasis thrusts itself / into the ink and suctions in near-silence." The reason why we do not see the mirage sharply, as the Sohrawardi quotation at the head of the volume tells us, may not be due to our sharp understanding but to the imperfection of our thirst. It is a nice conceit, illustrating what we need to bring to vision-making. In his sharpness, his seriousness and his extravagant arabesques, Galway Kinnell creates a satisfying oasis in contemporary poetry.

C. D. Wright's *String Light* is a prismatic poetry, catching the light in a random, tangential fashion. The tone of some of her lyrics recalls the simplicity of Ezra Pound's Chinese translations such as "The River Merchant's Wife":

I sit in the shade drinking ice water
When I bend to pick up your paper against the fence
it blows into the brown stalks of the cosmos;
I can feel you leaning back on your heels
chewing on the good times and the bad.

The poetic path leads from Pound through her native Ozarks to the contemporary American woman. C. D. Wright has traveled it successfully. Her poems pick up their feet neatly; they are witty and assured; they draw on a woman's world and have a continual oddity which makes us watch them with interest. All poems have linguistic slippages within them. Wright skirts this edge and her poems do not always yield their "sense" easily. Here is a not unfairly chosen extract from "Our Dust":

I had registered dogs 4 sale; rocks, dung and straw
I was a poet of hummingbird hives alone with redheaded stepbrothers.

The reader fills in the gaps and adds to the story. The poet probably does have redheaded stepbrothers and hummingbird hives. The lines can be taken literally. As an abstract painter said, "What you see is what you get." Such poetry has wide freedoms. It is private and quirky, making small, unexpected explosions inside our normal linguistic fortress. In spite of her cosmopolitan stance, Wright writes of ordinary life, particularly the life of the American woman. In "Self Portrait on a Rocky Mount," she declares:

I am the goat. Caroline by name. Née 6 January. Domesticated since
the 6th century before Jesus, a goat himself.
We have served as a source of meat, leather, milk and hair. Our flesh is
not widely loved. Yet our younger, under parts make fine gloves.

She concludes:

> We are sure-footed, esp. on hills. We live on next-to-nothing. This week's victuals: ironing-board covers and swollen paperbacks. Our small hills of filings fall under the heading of useful by-products. This we call Industrial Poetry. Both of us being Bearded, Mystic, Horned.

C. D. Wright is a poet who repays concentration: sure-footed as her goat, her poems are selections from events – elegant, witty and contemporary. They jump from rock to rock with diagonal leaps and we need to keep our eye on where they are going.

Kathleen Fraser's four long poems on Italian life and history beginning with the Etruscans are written in the postmodernist fashion. For those unfamiliar with the tradition that stems from Olson, Black Mountain and Creeley and perhaps the language poetry (Creeley and Olson are mentioned in a letter), the devices may appear pretentious. They are certainly not unique to this poet. The quotation marks, deletions, erasures, marginalia, cut-off words and phrases, drawings of Etruscan letters, insertion of real letters, private references and other typographical oddities including Giotto's perfect circle may be justified in the context of an uncertain, hesitant culture that unites the Romans with us. Of the four sections ("Etruscan Pages"; "Frammenti Romanti"; "Giotto: Arena"; and "when new time folds up"), the Etruscan section is the most accessible. The scholarly and archaeological material is matched by the fragmentary and evanescent. D. H. Lawrence's comment on Giotto which prefaces the volume is as illuminating as anything else: "(He) seemed to have been a flowering again of the Etruscan blood, which is always putting forth a flower and always being trodden down again by some superior force." Kathleen Fraser does not aim for such syntactical coherence and perhaps she is right. Lawrence could be as totalitarian as the Romans; the poet here records (the first section of the final poem) a fleeting, unpublic view of a relationship:

understood and scrupulous

I would have stayed at home as

rehearsal

if a bystander plated in gold, food

understood and scrupulous among

metal bowls, but a doctor goes

to the Gymnasium where scale is
in key
brick to the heart and air com-

pletely empties itself, without

gender'd regard, thus I tried

my luck as "you", in neutral,

running with you as we talked,

inside the blue grape hyacinth
represses
where nature reproduces its

mechanical force, *rhugetta*

wild in tomb grass,

I find this a little too elliptical. Other readers will perhaps be more reconstructive. After all, Rome wasn't built in a day, and its destruction took even longer.

The two poles of American poetry seem to be represented at the present time by the followers of John Ashbery on the one hand and the descendants of Robert Lowell on the other. Around the first pole are grouped those poets for whom language breaks and reforms in non-referential patterns, whereas Stephen Rodefer writes in his preface to *Four Lectures*: "Deliberate decomposition is required in a state of advanced decay" – or where Lyn Hejinian rejects all ideas of closure. At the other pole are those descendants of Lowell's *Life Studies* and the fact-hugging colloquialisms of personal history. It is almost as if one is necessary as a shadow or *doppelgänger* of the other. Between the extreme abstractions of a poetry which rejects the visible recognizable world that linguistic signs attempt to capture and the poetry that grips it desperately with whitened knuckles, there is a curious connection.

David Mason's twelve-part narrative poem that takes up half of his volume is emphatically of the Lowell School, chronicling a family history from the Civil War through the two voices of Lieutenant Mitchell and his daughter, Maggie Gresham. The tone is deliberately as flat as the prairies which open the poem. There are banal phrases – "We were heading west" linked with images which struggle not to take off: "The snow had melted and everywhere it seemed / were bones like cages with no birds inside." This image can be taken as emblematic: the poet creates cages with no birds inside but we sense their absence and their vanished songs as we are also aware of the trembling and insubstantial nature of reality in the new world that the little girl sees as threatening:

I knew this fear would always follow me
wherever I went, that I was not real,
that no one really lived who bore my name.
The lamplit face upon the swaying glass
was all that I would ever know of truth.
When Mama snuffed the lamp, my other face
retreated to the land of passing shadows.

Alongside this discourse is the father's narrative of the Civil War. It, too, is spare, factual, with snatches of colloquialism ("It took me back, I don't mind telling you") and with a concrete immediacy that relies on quirky details such as the soldiers being more wounded by the bees whose hives they robbed than by the enemy Confederate soldiers. The "reality" of the Civil War emerges as eccentric, possibly authentic but also tangential, partial:

We got back safe with peaches, corn, honey,
hogs and brandy, halted where the Colonel
rode out to meet us behind the picket lines.
"Did you have any trouble, Mitch?" he says.
"Yes, Sir" I said, "we skirmished with some bees."
The men were a great sight, so badly stung
we had to laugh, but they ate well that night.

As readers we are aware of other realities in both these discourses, ranging from the official histories of the War to fictional representations such as Stephen Crane's *The Red Badge of Courage*, which Lieutenant Mitchell's account resembles. Between the Longfellow-reading young woman and the logistically-minded officer, there is the opposition of war and peace/male and female/escape and imprisonment. But there is also the opposition between the bald statement of facts and the possibility of other poetry which eschews representation altogether. The other poems in this volume show that David Mason has deliberately abandoned a more traditional lyricism as "In The Northern Wood" where a dead girl is found:

The wind that stripped the birches by the lake
dusted the first snow on her hollow gaze,
then warmed her slender limbs for no one's sake.
Hunters who found her stood by in a daze . . . .

The re-emergence of epic, story-telling poetry is a contemporary possibility alongside the oft-repeated assertions that "it is not the business of poetry to be anything." The use of soliloquies enables the poet/author to steer around the too-impressive finalities of the dominating poet. The fine line between being something and being nothing is caught in one stanza particularly well and it brings together the balancing act of the poem which on the one hand sets out to negotiate a series of historical events and on the other to create a linguistic event which is unique and new:

Who was I but the girl who read Longfellow
to her Papa when his war-damaged eyes
no longer focused on the page, and when
no men came by to listen to his stories?
My sisters loved the poets, too, but I
was the one who read aloud. I understood
always that I was here to be a voice.

JOHN DANIEL

LOON TERRITORY

Straight Out Of View, poems by Joyce Sutphen (Beacon Press, Boston, 106 pp., 1995; $12.95, paper).
The Long Experience of Love, poems by Jim Moore (Milkweed Editions, Minneapolis, MN, 1995, 95 pp.; $12.95, paper).
When The Italians Came to My Home Town, poems by Thom Tammaro (Spoon River Poetry Press, Box 6, Granite Falls, MN, 56241, 80 pp., 1995; $6.95, paper).
Minnesota Suite, poems by Thom Tammaro (Dacotah Territory Press, Box 931, Moorhead, MN, 56561, 1996, 24 pp.; $3, paper).
Ordinary Days, poems by Orval Lund (Dacotah Territory Press, Box 931, Moorhead, MN 56561, 1996; 27 pp., $3.50, paper).
Door to the River, poems by David Pink (Dacotah Territory Press, Box 931, Moorhead, MN 56561, 1996; 27 pp., $3.50, paper).

Joyce Sutphen grew up in Minnesota and she celebrates it in "Tornado Warning":

> This is not the country for poetry.
> It has no mountains, its flowers
> are plain and never poisonous,
> its gardens are packed into blue mason jars.
> There are no hedges bordering the roads, the sky
> flies up from ditches, loose in every
> direction.
> Yet I know it to be passionate . . . .

The black tornado returns at the end of the poem, "a black fist . . . as any blind heart know." I suspect this will be a popular volume, especially in Minnesota and the Midwest. It combines a recognizable emotional world. Traditional inform, based on an intimate knowledge of farm life, Sutphen's verve is of the new calf or work which "fed the animal in me" or peeling potatoes, but there is also a thread of the tornado there, lifting off from the mundane flatness of the prairie into the dark sky. At the end of a poem about her grandmother, "helpless until they found her, the jar / of canned fruit smashed on the cement," the poet combines the mason jars with the twister. In "Grand Canyon, Early December" the poet looks at a photograph of her former husband or lover balancing on the edge of the canyon ("Oh, if she had only taken this as a warning . . . .") and then moves on to the cataclysmic ending where the violence of the landscape is used to parallel the relationship:

> What meteor was it slammed its fiery fist
> into earth's smooth face? What terrible,
> titanic angel reclined his limbs
> in the slaking, new-made planet
> and beat his pinioned wings
> deeper and deeper into the rock?

Romantic, liberal and generous, Joyce Sutphen includes a somewhat predictable section of London: Holland Park, the British Museum, Dover Beach, and "On Reading Sylvia Plath" where we might have expected a fierce identification, as she was the winner of the 1994 Barnard New Women Poets Prize. But she simply asks "aren't we all to blame?" – and there is a sense of weariness and sadness spreading over the Unreal City. I prefer the more offbeat touches in her poetry, as in "Great Salt Lake": the "door handle breaking off in our hands / the brittle chrome of our first fears." They're worth a dozen Londons.

The Long Experience of Love, Jim Moore's most recent collection, takes its title from Rilke, but there is a second dedication more appropriate from Regina Wheat: "Loss is the most intimate language the world has with which to speak to us of love." The title poem describes the poet holding a photograph of his mother: "Our lives are small things, / easy to miss . . . . " The poet recalls a broken bird's egg he had showed her. Mothers "make it seem natural to love what ends." Many of the poems are about loss and death and a failure to communicate. There is an acknowledgment of this desolation in "Hold Up Winter":

> . . . . Hold up for everyone, the core
> beneath the leaves, the totem that is hidden
> under abundance . . . .

The volume is a series of poems centered around loss – the death of the poet's father, a sequence to a child who was never born, loneliness and a series of prose poems on being fifty. Buried in the center of the work is a poem entitled "With Timmy, In And Out Of Prison" – in which Moore recounts the story of his friendship with a young black man, a fellow prison inmate years earlier, the frightening element in that tenuous friendship, and how Timmy promised to visit him after they were both released, but never did.

Jim Moore comes near the confessional but never enters. His poems tend to be more assertive than exploratory. A fuller unwinding of the soul would be more interesting.

I have been taken to task by Mark Vinz for suggesting that too much Minnesota poetry is concerned with loons, Swedish grandmothers and the cruel art of fishing. Thom Tammaro's grandmother is Italian and he grew up in the steel-making valleys of western Pennsylvania, but since 1983 has taught at Moorhead State University where he is now Professor of Multidisciplinary Studies. As a result, he has been influenced by the Loon School of Poetry. Of his youth in Pennsylvania, Tammaro has some good stories to tell.

The first prose piece – "Innocent Traveler" – is about his grandparents in an Italian village and a murdered lover. It reminds one of John Berger's stories of Alpine France and that writer's describing himself as "death's secretary" recording a history which otherwise would not be written. In some of these tales, Tammaro is death's secretary. The narratives are below-the-surface stories of a working-class childhood in an Italian Catholic community. I especially liked those of the nuns' authoritarianism – such "Why God Gave Us Muscles" – and then "The Day Kennedy Was Shot" which depicts how children were forced to kneel on the floor, arms outstretched, holding textbooks so that their pain would assist the President in his struggle for life: "So there we were: seventy-two sagging arms, little soldiers of Christ, little crosses kneeling in the aisle of our Golgotha to save the President."

The title story records the complex history of the Italian immigrants who began as stonemasons before being compelled to enter the steel foundries as cheap labor. They are poignant stories, somewhat sentimental about Catholicism and America but vivid snapshots of a history off the main highway and the dominant myths of white America.

To be a member of the Loon School of Poetry, it is necessary to observe three rules. First, be obsessively concerned with the details of your family history, preferably Scandinavian and full of pot-bellied stoves and snow, and to expect other people to be the same. Second, be equally fascinated, if not obsessed, by lures, lakes and loons and memories of fishing with your father, or indeed memories of not fishing with him. Third, write like a social historian. Tammaro has been strongly influenced by the nest of singing loons in spite of his Pennsylvania childhood.

His chapbook, *Minnesota Suite*, is an *après la deluge* reprint after floods destroyed the 1989 Spoon River imprint. It is also definitely of the Loon School. "Closing The Cabin" has loons calling in the still afternoon;

there is "Fishing With My Father" – which also appears in the other volume and is about *not* fishing with his father. There are poems about snow. There is the social historian in a prose poem, "Thinking of Steinbeck and Charlie": "I am traveling west of US 10, the old east-west highway that originally connected Minneapolis-St. Paul to the rest of the state before the clean, pale concrete path of Interstate 94 ribboned its way through the Minnesota landscape."

Hiding in the loon's nest is a Chinaman, Po Li, an astronomer, and two poems which are Chinese in spirit: "Lyrics" and "Minnesota Suite" – akin to drops of clean water and quite beautiful:

VI
When
the years
come on
maybe
I'll lay
my pens
and books
aside.

VII
Float
on a
fisherman's
boat.

VIII
Maybe
I'll come
back to
this lake.

If everything else in Minnesota disappeared in the Flood except for the volumes of poetry published by Dacotah Territory Press at Moorhead State University, we would be left with an incomparable record of what it was like to live in Minnesota in the latter part of the twentieth century. Or would we? There is a remarkable consensus among these volumes: grandfathers and loons, fishing on the lakes, a male culture of hunting and arm-wrestling, a female culture of grandmother's cakes sprinkled with down-home memories of adolescents sporting themselves in parked cars. The mythic recipe extends to not-so ironic truth-telling, as if language could ever avoid sliding on the ice. Orval Lund's chapbook has a number of such instances. In "Stolen Bases," the poet has a moment of truth:

> Where have you gone, Mickey Mantle, Bill Martin.,
> my necessary enemies? My father and uncles were
> all Yankee fans, all merchant-Republicans,
> while I grew up Democrat and moved away.
> I'm a mangy, stray dog, loose in a field I don't belong.

There are vignettes of small-town life that often capture the community in a sentimental way as in the poem praising women teachers:

> Mrs. Wallenberg, with dark-brown matted wig,
> large bones and voice, ambitious
> for us beyond our parents, who pronounced
> the dictator of Russia *Krooz-choff*!

In "Men in Winter," Lund describes the male hunters and fishers in winter with untypical negativity. They are "sluggish as bullheads forty feet deep." Fishing, that *ne plus ultra* of the Minnesota culture, is presented as a ridiculous sport. Women on the other hand are entertaining and their talk is refreshing with gales of laughter. The end of the poem unexpectedly turns the gender tables with a neat pun in the final line: "God I love 'em. / The women. Who drive me out / onto the ice."

In "Abridged," there's a poem about a man who fastens names to things, exact names that give them status and meaning. "When an elm would die / he'd remove the sign, wait for volunteers / to spring up – *boxelder, mulbery, / black locust*." In the surrealistic fantasy that concludes the poem ("In his yard / I'm going to plant an unabridged dictionary"), Lund critiques the dominant realism in a lively fashion.

Door to the River by David Pink also covers the familiar Northern Minnesota ground but has some original strengths, too: the title poem takes off from the straight realism of a fishing trip to commemorate Camera Haines, a pike fisherman. The last two stanzas conclude with an authentic elegiac tone:

> The big pike followed after, swallowing stars
> Like flies, until all the lights
> Swam away in the Christmas sky.

That is why this night is black,
Because Camera Haines has gone fishing
And he won't be coming back.

In "Train Town," the poem describes a town tormented by clanking boxcars and a man cut in half by the train who is cursed, not mourned, by the townspeople; it too concludes with a memorable last line:

Train tortured,
Leaping out of bed,
To curse again
The dumb, stupid head.

David Pink at his best combines operatic richness with an awareness of mundane thinness. I like "Window Flower Box," especially the two middle verses where he zooms in on the African violets:

Now we've left, where we're going; we know so well there's
Nowhere to get to. Moment by moment we cross across time,
a bow
Drawn over a cello. We'd like to aspire to a greater tragedy
than the day by day dregs of passionate emptiness: a punch in the nose.

Drunk stumble into a restaurant railing, slippery wet sex
in the sculpture garden, and the great fear that we'll never
be famous,
These window box African violets may be the closest we get
to exclamations of exotic tropics . . . .

In another poem, "Nightsweat," Pink speaks of "an obscene meat of tulips." We're a long way from Grandmother's home cooking and that's not a bad poetic thing, especially in Minnesota.

JOHN DANIEL

SIX POETS

Simplicity, poems by Ruth Stone. (Paris Press, Northampton, MA, 115 pp., 1995; $12.95, paper).
Her Slender Dress, poems by Susan Yuzna. (The University of Akron Press, Akron, Ohio, 73 pp., 1996; $12.95, paper).
Rush Hour, poems by Kevin FitzPatrick (Midwest Villages & Voices, Box 40214, Saint Paul, MN 55104, 82 pp., 1997; $9, paper).
The Lost Music, poems by Thomas R. Smith (The Bookpress, 101 South Main, River Falls, WI, 54022, 1996; 19 pp; $7.50, paper).
Growing Darkness, Growing Light, poems by Jean Valentine (Carnegie Mellon University Press, Box 21, Pittsburgh, PA 15213-3799, 1997; 70 pp., $20.95, paper; $11.95, paper).
In The Wind's Edge, poems by Ralph J. Mills, Jr. (Asphodel Press, distributed by Publisher's West Group, Box 8843, Emeryville, CA, 94662, 1997; $12.95, paper).

Born in 1915, Ruth Stone is now 85, although the photograph on the back cover of her leaning against a screen door could be that of a woman half that age. More importantly, her poetry has the alertness and complexity of the major modernists. The first verse of the first poem in the collection sets the tone:

> To you, born into violence,
> the wars of the red ant are nothing;
> you, in the heart of the eruption.

Here is contemporary America through the wrong end of the telescope with the urgency of a poet who has a message to convey. Ruth Stone is a poet who is unable to range from the surrealistic to the documentary and from a political fierceness to occasional verse about, for example, the plumber coming to repair the lavatory:

> even the day before that,
> in a moment of pure joy
> And instead of the awful stench
> of the day before and perhaps
> you smell nothing but the sweet
> mold of an old house
> and your own urine as it sloshes
> down with the flush.

And you feel comfortable, taken care of,
like some rich Roman matron
who has just been loved by a boy.

These are not nostalgic pieces of chopped-up domesticated prose chewed around in an academic maw. They include the recognizable world but are not of it. They delight in the sweep of language but don't take off entirely. They are aware of a woman's vision of the world and capable of linking to the cosmos, as in this opening to "The Mothers":

Working out of the mind, the wind says,
I take little or nothing.
I exchange one thing for another.
I rearrange.
Bother, the sand says,
she will not let me be,
slap, slap.

I cannot help it.
I have no bones of my own.
I am the mother of everything.
I am the lap of the world.
Dissolve in me, says the ocean.

At her best, Ruth Stone is an important poet. She is also an enjoyable poet, not easy but not grim, either, nor with that irritating twistedness that characterizes a number of contemporary writers. She relishes language. There is a happy, optimistic lilt to her work that taps into the basic creativity of things. One of my favorite poems goes from housework to outer space with the speed of light. Here it is in full – "Order and Design":

Compare the galaxy to a night of fireworks;
exploding phosphenes, mirror images.
Shine the house, rearrange furniture.
You are tracing mandalas lit inside the skull.
The calm and ordinary
is always based on a most delicate rite.
The chair placed on an unseen loop
of a circle, the housekeeper in the continuum
coming from deep within the brain
and departing at the speed of light.

Susan Yuzna's first volume, *Her Slender Dress*, the winner of the 1995 Akron Poetry Prize, speaks strongly about the troubled, wayward life of the 1960s-1970s literary intellectual, involved in the counter culture of drugs and rootless traveling. It also speaks strongly about being a woman. The feminist revolution came after the hippie phase and seems to have been responsible for rescuing Ms. Yuzna and pulling her on to the dry land of an instructorship at the University of North Dakota, but it is the earlier turmoils and traumas that supply the drama, that sense of a real abyss a million miles away from the safety of an English Department. The title poem begins arrestingly enough:

> The second time
> I saw Nureyev dance, I was on heroin

It is the heroin that prevents her shedding tears when Nureyev is presented with roses. "Heroin allows no tears, no fluids whatsoever, you can't even pee." But it fuels the transcendental lyricism that enables her to float high over the audience and to relish their elegance:

> The multicolored shirts, endlessly endearing,
> those silken scarves blowing in the wind.

It allows her to think she is God "serene and sexless" and to contemplate joining the immortals by slipping off her slender dress as the lioness had loosened the maid's dress in the Blake quotation that heads the poem. Yuzna writes about love – she makes the Ex an archetypal figure – and violence, frequently interweaving the two. The first picture of her going to the ballet remains with the reader throughout the volume:

> It was cold in Iowa but I was not cold
> in my slender dress, gold brocade with a fringe, black,
>
> a cheap affair, but the closest I could come
> to elegance in those days.

The vulnerability remains even if some of the poems such as "The Way of the Moth 11: At an Amtrak Station" posit a sexually active, fantasizing woman. Yuzna uses the full range of female response from the gold brocade to a gigantic male-consuming moth. But the realism is never far away:

> It strikes me as utterly appropriate
> they now sell high-priced denim outfits
> over the very spot
> where you beat me up.

Yet these are more than confessional poems, for there is always a surrealistic take-off or a lyrical moment or a sudden change of tone that lifts the poem from the heavy morass of the weighty and the confessional. There are also the references to Blake and Rilke and the whole cultural tradition which add another dimension. In "Meat and Potatoes," the narrator begins by peeling potatoes, wanders into a speculation based on her reading of a book about a Polish ghetto where the Jews queued for peelings, then into her father's meat-packing plant, and finally back to the sink. The one long, unbroken peeling and the suddenness of the final image bring the different aspects of her narrative together:

> I have done it, escaped the bad marriage.
> I will eat potatoes forever. Always, the price,
> I hear my friend say, as I drop the brown spiral
> into the disposal and grind it to mush.
> With the flip of a switch, a certain relish.
> How quick, the blades. Just noise.

Some of Yuzna's poems are rather long, carrying more themes than they can quite manage, so there is a sense of overloaded narrative. But there is a taut voice here, a lyrical sense, imaginative leaps and an agonizing sense of what violence and damage love can cause, hovering on the edge of madness. For Minnesotans, there is the Aristotelian plus of recognizing some of the places where love takes place:

> O, to lunch again
> at the Walker, to pour out my troubles,
> to be calmed by the loveliness of her face!

Poetry is carried along by its rhythms as much as by its words and Kevin FitzPatrick's characteristic rhythms embody the urge to tell a graphic story:

> The asphalt's wet but free of snow at last,
> and breathless boys contend at basketball,

trying to finish one more game real fast
despite a father's loud persistent call.
(from "Rude Life")

His poetry charts the familiar lives of those who live in the Twin Cities, centering on the public as well as the private, on those decisions we all make as citizens in addition to our inner dramas. In "Bearing Arms," for example, the woman who is accosted by a man learns to handle a gun although ultimately she decides not to fire it. In "Plane Crash," the DC-10 is compared imaginatively with swatting a silver bug in the kitchen. Inevitably, FitzPatrick's depiction of the contemporary American scene concentrates on bizarre moments of violence such as the time when a 70-year-old woman with purple hair almost runs him down:

From the rearview mirror
of her pink mint-condition
'57 Chevy swings
a serene male religious figure
wildly by his neck.
As she descends,
a final message heralds,
GOD IS COMING AND SHE IS PISSED.

Such moments of observation are characteristic starting points for many of these poems, incidents which spark a surge of emotion or a connecting link with another image. FitzPatrick's poetry is a strong reaction to external stimulus, a kind of poetic journalism which seeks to connect the outer world with the inner, as we all must. It is also poetry of the locality – Saint Paul and the demolition of the Nicols, Dean and Gregg building – the Catholic background – Lake Superior – the Unemployment Office. He captures the seedy, downtown life of Minnesota slush and snowbanked sidewalks. There is a fascination with the mundane and the ordinary, encapsulated in the portrait of the worker in the chicken factory:

I stand all day
and bone chickens.
I've done this for years –
dump the meat on one belt,
the bones on another,
to carry them away.
I'm only fifty-three

but my feet are all sores
from diabetes and the floor
wet with running water.
My doc says to quit
while I'm still walking.
("To Whom It May Concern")

This is a poetry which is accessible and ultimately political in the wider sense. As such, it is a welcome arrival at a time when poetry too rarely concerns itself with the visible and the public. There is a danger, of course, which prevents poets today assuming the bardic persona of those in earlier times. The depiction of the external is never unproblematic. Words can be as slippery as Saint Paul sidewalks. Kevin FitzPatrick might take cognizance of their movement rather more than he has done. Still, like Aristotle, we all rejoice in recognition of the known, and any poet who has lived through a Minnesota winter will understand the relief of "the asphalt's wet but free of snow at last" as he (or she) bounces the poetic basketball.

Thomas R. Smith's elegantly produced volume is a chapbook containing a dozen poems centered around River Falls in Wisconsin. In a note in the back of the collection, Smith writes: "When I first arrived in River Falls as a college freshman in September, 1966, the feature of the town I loved most was the Kinnickinnic River, the South Fork of which slid over its rocky bed less than a block from my dormitory room." The poems here are celebrations of nature. "Summer Morning" captures the particularlity of walking and expands into a lyric joy:

Bits of wet straw cling to my bare feet.
All things that live follow the paths of desire.
All who walk on a summer morning walk on water.
(from "Summer Morning")

This desire is caught again in a fine prose poem, "Maple Seeds":

They twirl down in May wind, heavy noses aimed at upended in grass. Their job is to pierce like tiny darts, slice through leaves to reach their target, blunt fins will fail, blunt fins upended in grass.

Most will fail, but their failing helps a few succeed. The maple race goes on. Both are the tree: the gigantic wooden structure each downed flyer knows how to

build, and also this community of desire scattered in the
shade.

Elsewhere Smith can become a little wistful when he recalls a lost relationship or he can veer into cliché and provincial sermonizing with lines like "the secret that has given him his life" after vividly describing a coyote:

a coyote stands in perfect stillness,
watching the stiff, rat-tracked grass
(from "Driving Through Custer National Park")

In America, the world's most urbanized culture, Thomas R. Smith can ignore the cities and the media and at his best create a world that is still meaningful, complete and poignantly lyrical as in the short poem, "In Late Winter":

The frozen lake never loses its patience
with winter. On an appointed day in April
the loon will meet its reflection in open water.
Imagination opens again to earth. We
believe in bees, the wild rose's grail filled
with summer. The watery twin comes nearer.

Jean Valentine's new book is her seventh. She won the Yale Younger Poets Competition back in 1965 with her first collection, *Dream Barker*. Her new collection contains difficult, elliptical poems, although they are rarely longer than ten lines. A clue to their provenance is the quotation from Joseph Bruchac's *Survival This Way, Interviews with American Indian Poets*, where Lance Henson's words (from which the title poem is taken) suggest that the light between darkness and dawn embodies transition, and that this crossing-over is also found in dreams. The initial poem, "Rain," captures this interweaving of water and light in the image of snakes running down the window – "their heads full of light" – "earth wet on your mouth" – the two elements fused in the image rather than in the actuality of raindrops. So the images float precariously into the poems like targets into the crosshairs of sights, sometimes with a clear beauty:

Leonardo's man in the circle, but a woman,
the circle adrift in the middle of the lake:
cross through the line someone, salmon or hawk.

The rowboat drifts
on this northern evening's midnight's line of light,
green lip reflecting lip,
and I float in it,
salt, and breath, and light,
hawk and salmon and I . . .

(from "Homesick")

The North Woods? Leonardo's image? Light is important to Jean Valentine, as in this more easily understood poem, which I imagine is about Ireland where she lives half of each year:

The tractors at night,
the dimly lighted
kindly lobsters
with glass sides,
with men inside,
and at home, wives,
and depression's black dogs
walking out of
the January hedges'
hacked-off sides.

("The Tractors")

The ungainly lurching of the tractors and the massacre of the January hedges are visual and emphatic. Elsewhere the poet is more obscure with sudden switches of tone. This is perhaps her characteristic form, the abrupt cross-cutting of question, as in "Where Do You Look for Me?" – in memory of James L. White, the Minnesota poet who died in 1981:

They think because I am dead now
I am no longer twigs on the ground,
stone or bits of stone in the wall.
That I was just something good on a plate
for them to eat. That I have no one.

Oh my darling,
where do you look for me?

The tone of Valentine's poetry here is elegiac, full of death and dissolving, tense and on the edge of a paper-thin skin, as this section of "Open Heart":

> Your shy body, turned
> to silk and bone, thin blue silk
> coat for what water. . .

Jean Valentine's poetry is tentative, finely honed, whittled down to a flint-like hardness, a stay against sentimentality and the indulgence of those who wallow in emotion. As such, it seems like poetry that has been hard fought for and worth holding up to the light as one might hold up a flint to see what shines through or what lies inside.

Since Ezra Pound's invention of Imagism was the beginning of the century and his celebration of the Chinese ideogram, American poets have looked to the East as well as the West for inspiration. The fascination with the spare, condensed style of eastern art has offered an alternative to the hectic, emotional bustle of the western tradition and the eastern influence emerges throughout the century in the work of William Carlos Williams, Charles Olson, the Black Mountain and Objectivist poets and here in the poetry of Ralph J. Mills, Jr. His poems resemble Japanese brush paintings: delicate swirls laid immediately but precisely onto the paper:

> grey
>   green
>
> ice on
> the pond water –
>   snow not
> thick or
> fast-falling
>   sifts like a
> persistent drizzle
>
>   /
>   willow
>
>   wands toss
> as the wind
> begins

: cherry, ash
tree
pull back

& gather –

("Grey/Green")

Unlike poems in the western tradition, there is no thumping closure but a tentative breaking-off as if the poet had simply paused. The effect is to suggest that life or nature goes on and is not enclosed in the rigid frame of the artist's construction. The ongoing flow is indicted by dashes or slashes with a lone colon directing our attention away from the willow to the cherry and ash. The success of this poetry lies primarily in the sense of importance which it brings to the smallest details. A branch moves and that is important. The poet makes you feel that something significant is happening which you may have refused to watch or been too busy to notice. This is his twelfth book of poetry and Mills retains the freshness of vision which makes his work a rejoicing of nature:

out where snow's
streaking like
a quickened
white wing –

For ultimately it is not the Objectivist School or the influence of the Japanese brush paintings that make these poems of Ralph Mills effective but their capturing of freshness in nature. Wind, shadows and rain impart a sense of movement which enables us to see the natural world in miniature like a bonsai tree and to step aside from the avalanche of contemporary action. The words are simple but arresting with the freshness of a rainwashed sky.

JOHN DANIEL

THE MUSE OF EUGENE J. McCARTHY

And Time Began, poems by Eugene J. McCarthy (Lone Oak Press, 304-11th Ave. S.E., Rochester, MN, 55904, 47 pp., 1993; $10, paper).
Selected Poems, by Eugene J. McCarthy (Lone Oak Press, Rochester, MN, 155 pp., 1997; $14.95, hardback).

Eugene J. McCarthy, a one-time candidate for the Presidency, most notably in 1968, and a former U.S. Senator from Minnesota, was one of those politicians who promised hope in a desperate world. The fact that he was defeated only made his career more poignant, linked with those Americans whose names will always be associated not only with lost elections but lost causes. This volume (originally published back in 1968) has an elegiac tone, as in "Jumping Ship":

> With the wounds of Greece
> you have wounded us.
> You have wounded us with the deep sound
> of women crying out of centuries
> and with the shallow silence
> of the buried reed.

In "The Heron," there is a metaphysical twist that refashions the image into glory:

> The heron strikes and kills his wish
> For he eats only golden fish.
> And that same fish, mirrored
> In the heron's avid eyes
> Sees himself as golden and dies
> In that belief. Both fish and bird
> By the same sun, at last betrayed.

Perhaps McCarthy might select an epitaph from his long poem about his boyhood in Minnesota:

> The day was a kite
> I flew it on a string, winding
> it in to see its blue again . . . .
> (from "The Day Time Began")

Accompanying the poems are excellent black-and-white photographs of grasses, shorelines and storm-lit trees by Harry W. Schwarm.

In *Selected Poems*, there is an overall view but particular details in the chaotic world of war and suffering. There is a poignant and witty poem on the disappearance of Kilroy from Vietnam:

Kilroy
the unknown soldier
who was the first to land
the last to leave,
with his own hand has taken his good name
from all the walls and toilet stalls

Kilroy
whose name around the world
was like the flag unfurled
has run it down
and left Saigon
and the Mekong
without a hero or a song
and gone
absent without leave
from Vietnam

But McCarthy has a wider range from the immediate and the topical. In an elegy entitled "The Death of Vernon Watkins While Playing Tennis," McCarthy pays tribute to a poet he admires:

Vernon Watkins, near wanderer,
your voice careful as shadows,
a night wind among dry oats,

your voice, a gloved hand turning
gulls on updrafts above
the reaching estuary

and in the last verse:

Tennis was not your game.
Dressed in divers colors, Vernon,

why did you play the woman
in white?

In "10 Commandments" (shouldn't all poets write theirs?), I particularly liked numbers 6 and 7:

6. Do not look long on a harbor
   from which all ships are gone

7. Speak always as though children
   were listening

And in "The Heron," the poet combines a genuine feeling for nature with a metaphysical wit that makes his work enjoyable to read:

Why does the heron wait
Alone, controlled, celibate?
Simon Stylites on his rod
Looking for the weakening of God,
The executioner who prays
A day before he slays.

There have not been many British or American politicians who have been able to write as well as Eugene McCarthy and not many whose politics were as good, either.

JOHN DANIEL

LESLIE ADRIENNE MILLER'S SECOND BOOK OF POEMS

Ungodliness, poems by Leslie Adrienne Miller (Carnegie Mellon University Press, Pittsburgh, 58 pp., 1994; $10.95, paper).

Readers familiar with Leslie Adrienne Miller's first book, *Staying Up For Love* (Carnegie Mellon, 1990), will recognize some of the subjects that reappear in *Ungodliness*: men, God, family, and childhood. The central issue in both collections is how much "trouble" it is to be an unconventional woman who displays the characteristics of a "difficult and stoic mother." Without self-pity, Miller's poems are witty and lyrical. She achieves a tone of intimacy without sacrificing a mastery of irony and craft.

The twenty-five poems in this collection are divided into three sections. Most of the poems are a little over a page and progress with a loose iambic beat. Focused and densely imagistic, Miller's poems work well within primarily non-stanzaic structures. She begins the second section with "Child Mottled Man, Woman Attached" – a sensuous and philosophical poem employing a difficult form, the *canzone*. Perhaps this is the poet's way of suggesting that she has studied poetic traditions, earning her choice to express herself in free verse. She also has a wry sense of humor, her poems replete with wicked details. In "Police Tent at the County Fair," she succeeds with a ruthless and rhythmically flawless poem that celebrates human absurdity. Here are the first and then the closing lines:

> My father's name was everywhere that summer,
> on nail files, combs, pencils and buttons
> free at the table in the Republican tent.
> I sat in the August dust under the table
> with Judge Hixon's daughter. We counted
> matchbooks in the hot part of the day . . . .
>
> Even now I sometimes smile at cruel
> news, and I still don't know
> where it comes from – that flinching
> at the corners of the mouth when one body
> suddenly and fully comprehends the end of another.

Another poem is about an eighth-grade English teacher taunted by her students who feel outrage that "she'd had / a baby but not a husband." But most of Miller's poems resonate with frightening concepts. Some explore sexual ambivalence: "Have been a good-at-saving-myself woman, / pushing the gossamer threads of sexual attachment / down my thighs . . . . " And "Impasse" – the final poem of the book – suggests an educated and privileged woman trading sexual favors for vacations with scenic views:

> I've gone away at summer's end
> with a few new mountains, merely borrowed
> from men who lived on them. I've stood
> on their porches not wanting them
> to touch me, and knowing they would anyway,
> so I could claim the view as my own.

Miller is willing to delve into her "ugly side." What makes this so fulfilling is the technical virtuosity she displays. The subjects are about situations the "I" lives with inwardly, outwardly, and awkwardly. The poet gives us compelling glimpses of the world and says, "Remember how interesting all of it is."

Ungodliness is a major achievement. Other significant poems are: "The Driving Range," "The Queen of Fortune," "On Looking at Photographs of My Grandmother's Old Boyfriends" and "Swimming with Horses." Leslie Adrienne Miller is a poet to read for the love of good poetry, both substantial and nurturing.

DINA BEN-LEV

A NATION OF WATCHERS

The Sibling Society, by Robert Bly. (Addison Wesley, New York, 1996, 302 pages; hardback, $25; Vintage Books, 1997; paper, $13).

The two voices of Robert Bly in *The Sibling Society*, and also to a certain extent in *Iron John*, present a difficulty for the reviewer. Bly is a magnificent poet with a clear and humane voice. He is a skilled translator, a wonderful, funny and compelling teller of stories and illuminator of myths. This voice – the voice of the poet – is one which speaks to us with great thunder and reverberation.

The other voice – a voice trying to apply the metaphors and images to modern society and its problems – is sometimes unclear, and prone to sweeping statements which defy meaning. "These smoky scenes in movies during which the eyes promise each other twenty years of hopeless desire are no longer filmed. The great romantics, such as Clark Gable, shrink to boys like Kevin Costner." One can agree that the "do all, show all" aspect of modern films has all but eradicated passion of the screen, but why does that make Gable a man and Costner a boy? And in the confusing sections of the book, in between the myths and stories, seems to be the voice of a man who is still working out his ideas, a voice thinking out loud. Writing in the voice of one who is still formulating concepts is probably dangerous to clarity and decisiveness.

One suspects that this duality is in great part the reason why Bly's books are often criticized by both professional critics and the reading public, particularly women. We are never quite sure what he means. So the reader goes to the easy interpretation: Bly wants men to be "real men" made of iron, women to be feminine and children to do as they are told. Nothing could be further from the truth, of course. Bly even says in this new volume that his earlier book, *Iron John*, was greatly misunderstood by critics: "I hadn't realized how many misunderstandings are possible in a single book when one speaks in myth form . . . . Most reviewers followed obediently the flat, literal or sociological mode, in which there is only one world – this one." The problem is trying to apply the myths in a "thinking-it-through" mode. The problem is readers who have not been taught to "read" the myths.

Mythological writing and interpretation utilize vertical, not horizontal, thinking – and explore all the possibilities and symbolisms inherent in the myth form. "Mythology doesn't deal in either/or, but both/and." Bly believes that one of the major by-products of the Sibling Society is the destruction of vertical thinking, which has been replaced by the narrowed focus of horizontal thinking. Vertical thinking is the thought process of artists, of any creative thinker and problem solver. Vertical thinking allows us to plunge into the atavistic brain, to revel in our dreams, to travel to the subconscious and return with new ideas, new images, new understandings. If we only think and view the world horizontally, we never see the possibilities.

In *The Sibling Society*, Bly warns us that "The superego or Interior Judge has altered its requirements. An Interior Judge that once demanded high standards in art, in writing, and in ethics now requires early success, at twenty or twenty-two. Those insistent on early success have devastated the art world." And, according to Bly, the world in general. We no longer move from childhood, to adolescence, to adulthood, accepting with each level of growth a new set of responsibilities, but rather we maintain our foothold in adolescence, judging our lack of success with furious intensity and violence. "The idea that our Interior Judge has changed its demands from requiring us to be good to requiring us to be famous is very sobering," Bly writes. "If superego, detached from verticality and stretched out across the horizontal plane, truly has changed, it means that consumer capitalism's dependence on stimulating greed and desirousness has changed something fundamental inside the human being, a result that Freud never anticipated."

This "society of want" is a major factor in the development of Bly's Sibling Society and is one in which the lack of instant gratification instills permanent sibling envy and rivalry in all its members. Since our society no longer seems to have a definition of adult behavior or has much respect for what has gone before, we look to what is essentially a mirror for our behavior patterns. There are no adults in sight. Children see their own reflection in the behavior of their peers. The ego-centered adolescent sees no higher level to achieve and therefore remains a sibling, fighting with brothers and sisters for the most, the best, the popular. Where is this desire for fame, this greed, this contempt for all that is not ego-satisfying coming from? Lacking strong parenting, children have turned to The Giant in the living room – Television.

I don't want to give the impression that Bly is holding up television as the cause of society's ills, but he does focus on television as a major metaphor. His concern is still firmly rooted in the place where family should stand – mothers and fathers, grandparents, aunts and uncles and all members of the extended family of the human race. We have turned away from the responsibility of raising children by all becoming members of a society of siblings. We have brought the patriarchal society down, but we haven't found a workable replacement. We are all a part of this destruction. We have left great gaps in our cultural paradigm and have filled the voids with the familiar voices of the screens.

Bly's arguments are sound and well supported by statistics, some scientific data and most interestingly by his interpretation of several fairy tales. The Giant of course appears in *Jack and the Bean Stalk*. The Giant represents for Bly "isolation and deprivation." The Giant in the fairy tale ". . . . eliminates the father first, which our society has already accomplished. The mother and children, spared for a while, are in great danger. Children particularly have to hide . . . . We don't realize that when we put a computer or television in a child's own room, we are sending that child to be alone with the Giant."

The portrait of our modern society which Bly draws is one in which the children are orphaned, left on their own, watching television and chatting on The Net – influenced not by the stories and histories of the families and the elders of their communities, not by the natural world, nor by the progression through civilized behavior which should guide them to adulthood – but by the ever-present glowing screens. The giant screens urge them to want, to buy, to possess material goods as a measure of success, and ultimately, a measure of their own worth. The screens show the violence, the mediocrity, the baseness of our society long before they are able to process the information. Millions of children, following the example set by millions of adults, are sitting in rooms watching a one-way communication, or typing on a screen "talking" to someone who may or may not be who he or she claims to be.

Aside from the destruction of socialization skills and the increase in violence, which are, Bly believes, attributable to the formation of this adolescent Sibling Society, Bly also posits that there has been a major change in the way our brains function and, ergo, in the way we learn. The process of creation has often been described as a rising and falling process. The mind plunges into the abyss of the subconscious and rises to the surface to tell others what it saw. The vision is painted, drawn, sculpted, written, or composed, and the audience takes the representation and essentially repeats the process individually. Bly believes that since we have become a society or horizontal thinkers, we no longer have the need or the skill to think vertically. The majority of images which we see are already in complete form: on television, primarily. Reading, of course, requires imagination on the part of the reader, but we seldom read. Art in any form is rarely taught in modern schools and very few members of our society actually go to museums, theaters, and concert halls. Bly insists that the Giant Screens have also had a negative effect on artists. They, too, are siblings and are not able to make the journey required of them as artists because their vertical thinking skills have been diminished. They are unable to take the plunge into the subconscious and therefore their art is not as rich and filled with nuance as it might be. The artists are a product of their time as is the art itself, and both have entered into the horizontal existence of the Sibling Society.

"Looking at the decline in discipline, inventiveness, persistence, reading abilities, and reasoning abilities of adolescents now compared with adolescents thirty years ago," Bly suggests, "we must be ready to grasp how much steeper the decline will be thirty years from now. As these children, who mistake Herbert Hoover for the maker of the vacuum cleaner, become directors of movies, critics of literature, curators of museums, and high school teachers, we will see a drop in coherence all across the board." Thus the circle is completed. Art reflects society, society reflects art – the eternal conundrum.

The first sentence paraphrase of this book ("It's the worst of times, it's the best of times.") perhaps should have come from *Bleak House* instead of *A Tale of Two Cities*. Yet in this sentence is a key to what is wrong with the book's thesis. Bly presents the worst of times with frightening clarity. But he has essentially left out the best of times. He is clear about what we have left behind – our true male and female selves, honoring our pasts, respecting our elders, caring for and guiding our children. His definitions of the worst parts of our society, which he describes as sibling, are very compelling, but the best of times as he describes them are in the past. It is possibly a reactionary stance.

We are a technological society and a fragmented society. We have potential for greatness, but we have lost our way. How do we apply the myths, the stories, the fairy tales to our society as it exists now? How do we cherish our elders when they are shut away in nursing homes or when there is no family at all, much less an extended one? How do we teach our children gentleness and respect and honor when we feel none of it in our workplaces or neighborhoods? How do children learn from nature when the only trees we see are dying from urban pollution? How do experience the communal joy of theater or music or poetry readings when going to a video store to rent a movie tape is as close to the artistic community as one gets? How do teachers illuminate myths when they must spend most of their teaching time seeking the attention of their students who are disrespectful, arrogant and fearful? How do we apply the lessons of myths when survival is the daily goal of so many members of our society?

Bly answers metaphorically when he urges us to stand the children and adults in a field facing one another and have each adult pull a child over to the adult side. If his view of society is a valid one, then there are no adults left. "The hope lies in the longing we have to be adults," Bly writes. By acting like adults, we might find that we have really become adults. He has a strongly held belief in the importance of the past and therefore we need "perception to understand that the world belongs primarily to the dead, and we only rent it from them for a little while." But he also acknowledges that the present is a new place, due in great part to the dismantling of "Power Hierarchies." Thus Bly writes: "It's as if all this has to be newly invented, and the adults then have to imagine as well what an elder is, what the elder's responsibilities are, what it takes for an adult to become a genuine elder."

Returning to the notion of duality of voices in *The Sibling Society*, the problem is not just Bly's tendency to "think out loud" or our shortsightedness as readers. Too many of us are no longer able to understand the language of myth. It is a once ready-at-hand skill that we've lost, just as we have lost our histories. Bly pinpoints this problem: vertical thinking is a required tool and we think horizontally. But the question still remains: how do we relearn these skills? We have been presented with the problem, and with the reason why it exists. But what is the answer?

As one of the elders, Robert Bly continues to try and teach us to read and apply the myths. His world is the world of images, reflections and metaphors, but with *Iron John* and now with *The Sibling Society*, he has entered a world which demands concrete answers. Are *Iron John* and *The Sibling Society* in need of an elder? Perhaps in a third book, such an elder might appear. One hopes he will help us find a way to be examples again and pull a vulnerable child into a new paradigm.

CAMILLE D'AMBROSE

INDIGENOUS VOICES

Messengers Of The Wind: Native American Women Tell Their Life Stories, edited by Jane Katz (Random House, 317 pp. 1995; New York: hardback, $23; Ballantine Books, New York; paper, $12).

Messengers Of The Wind is an appropriate title for Jane Katz's compilation of taped and transcribed interviews with American Indian women. The wind is hard to know. It is somehow always there, resting in the branches of the trees, in the waves of the lakes and seas, in the eddies of leaves blowing on the path, in the corridors of skyscrapers and high rises. It can bring the fires of the Santa Ana mountains, the tornado, the hurricane, or a cool relief from the heat of weather, insects or spiritual pain. It seems at times that the wind can pull down a mountain, turn placid water into a churning inferno and then soothe all back to foothills and crystalline brooks.

The wind as metaphor is a longstanding literary tradition. In *Messengers Of The Wind*, it is the culture, the tradition of the Indian Nation. The wind of the title has remained with the Indian nations throughout history, passed on from generation to generation. Katz has transcribed the life stories of Native women from all parts of the country. The stories are loosely woven into six major chapters. In the first section, the voices of women from New Mexico to Alaska speak to the transition from past to present and how the Native American cultures have both endured and changed during that journey. Led by traditions, ceremonies and a commitment to the land and the community, these women find themselves walking the trail from yesterday to today.

Soge Track lives in Taos, New Mexico, where she grew up. She is a potter who tells the story of her family and people with humor and respect. "My life today is so different from my mother's life . . . . I feel that you should be independent . . . .the men in my life haven't always agreed." Although Soge Track has traveled widely throughout the United States, France and Cuba, she has found her home right back where she began. "When I plant my garden," she opines, "I give an offering to Mother Earth . . . . it's almost a meditation. . . .I'm living the way I was raised. Living my life in this place is a ceremony of survival."

Subsequent chapters introduce women who reflect upon government policies which have displaced whole nations, despoiling both land and people in an effort of "relocation and re-education." Elaine Salinas was born on the White Earth Reservation in Minnesota. She now works at the

Urban Coalition in Saint Paul. "There were so many losses for women," she tells Katz. "There were cases in South Dakota where contaminated water caused abortions and premature births. A number of Indian women were sterilized – it happened across the country. Children were taken away from their mothers. Collectively, we lost so much."

The women recall the horrors of being uprooted from the security of home and community to be stripped of language, cultural and religious beliefs in a Christian community which was neither community nor Christian. Children were forbidden to speak their native languages and were pronounced "heathen" if they practiced their own religious and spiritual beliefs. Several of the women tell of verbal, physical and sexual abuse at the hands of those who were supposed to be teaching and nurturing them.

The women speak to the divisions within the Indian communities – divided by differing views of how to maintain the honor and sovereignty of the nations and yet survive politically and economically in the world today. Laura Wittstock, from the Cattaraugus Seneca Reservation in upstate New York, comes from a family of political activists. Her mother was active in the American Indian Movement (AIM), having taken part in the occupation of Alcatraz prison. Laura Wittstock is a writer who is also active in politics. She joined AIM in the early 1970s. "There was potential for corruption within the tribal governments," she explained to Katz. "There were fights for seniority, some of the leaders drank, media attention was seductive and they became `stars´ – that clouded their thinking." Wittstock now directs MIGIZI, a national network of Indian journalists. She now thinks ". . . of AIM as a phalanx, plowing the ground in order to meet the needs of our community. Its strength is that it has been able to change with the times." She speaks with eloquence about the enduring strength of her people: "Despite the battering of our traditions through the centuries, we have been strong enough to avoid extermination, to continue as a nation, to continue our government and salvage our identity. We still aspire to the ideals of the Iroquois Nation."

As each woman tells her story, philosophies of child rearing, community cooperation and growth, ecology, economics, religion and art are revealed. Ramona Bennett, a former chairperson of her tribe, the Puyallup, describes Indian communities: "Everybody knew the rules for social conduct, so there was no confusion. Everybody was useful and part of the future, so there was no need for unemployment insurance or welfare, juvenile detention centers, prisons or nursing homes. These Indians had extended families – the finest form of social security there is."

Virginia Poole is part of the Seminole Tribe and lives in Florida in a traditional village. "White people are changing the channels of the rivers," she observes. "They put roads where the rivers used to flow. They dig canals, and put up levees. When Lake Okeechobee is low in one area, people come around and tear down some of the levees so they'll have higher water in another area. . . .To me it's destructive. You're changing the whole ecological system. . . .We don't own land. We don't buy or sell land. That's always been prohibited. Nobody owns the land. We said we'd watch over it, because that's our responsibility. You just take care of the land, and it takes care of you."

Vi Hilbert of the Upper Skagit tribe in the Puget Sound area of Washington State is the storyteller and an honored elder of her tribe. She travels often to speak on ecological issues: "If you study what the Creator has put here on earth, you will learn many things. The earth has much to teach us. The way a blade of grass grows, the way the salt water, streams and rivers talk to us, the way the wind acts upon the waters and upon the trees, the way the clouds drift in the sky – these things are stories that you can study and learn from."

Jane Katz, as she writes in her introduction, felt ". . . .ethically bound to set down their stories faithfully." Her goal is accomplished with empathy and style. There is great reverberation in the musings and storytelling of these women. They are self-sufficient and opinionated. They work with vigor, stamina and humor. They keep an eye on the wind, and whenever possible they use it to forage lives for themselves, their children, their nations and the earth.

It must be said that all cultures have winds which follow them through history. My immigrant grandparents from Italy and Ireland all carried with them the traditions of the countries where they were born. My grandmothers in particular knew about the wind. Reading a book such as *Messengers Of The Wind* is a complex experience. On the one hand, there is much empathy here. All of the rituals, the day-to-day wisdom of the ages, the lessons, the healing, the prayers are familiar to those of us with grandparents such as mine, who held and passed on the richness of their beliefs. On the other hand, as part of the culture which ripped the sacred land and the rituals and the future from the hands of the indigenous peoples, it is difficult to read *Messengers Of The Wind* without sorrow. One can only feel gratified for the strength of the American Indian Nations and the power of the wind.

CAMILLE D'AMBROSE

SILENT OVER AFRICA

Dared and Done: The Marriage of Elizabeth Barrett and Robert Browning, by Julia Markus (New York: Alfred A. Knopf, 1995; 382 pp., 85 illustrations, hardback, $30).

They were an item worthy of "Ripley's Believe It or Not!" Two of England's greatest poets in the nineteenth century were of African-American descent! And not only that, their marriage was a glorious success! As Miriam Schaefer says in Hawthorne's *The Marble Faun*, their marriage was the "heroic union of two high, poetic lives!" They were Elizabeth Barrett (1806-1861) and Robert Browning (1812-1889), the authors of the verse novels *Aurora Leigh* and *The Ring and the Book*.

This genealogical conjecture, propounded in Julia Markus's *Dared and Done: The Marriage of Elizabeth Barrett and Robert Browning*, is not new. In 1890, Frederick James Furnivall found what Markus calls "much circumstantial evidence that Margaret Tittle, Browning's grandfather's first wife, had black blood." Furnivall notes that Robert Browning's father "was so dark that when, as a youth, he went out to his Creole mother's sugar-plantation in St. Kitts, the beadle of the Church ordered him to come away from the white folk among whom he was sitting, and take his place among the coloured people." There in the West Indies, Markus writes, "the system was deplorable to Robert Browning, Senior . . . .When he returned to England, he renounced his inheritance, to the eternal displeasure of his father."

As for Elizabeth, who also had a dark complexion, Robert Russa Moton claims in *What the Negro Thinks* (1929) that "it is carefully recorded that highly creditable records associate the names of Pushkin, Dumas, Elizabeth Barrett Browning, and even our own Alexander Hamilton with the Negro race." In *The Family of the Barretts* (1938), Jeannette Marks ripostes, "Dumas and Robert Browning, yes! Elizabeth Barrett, no! On the Barrett side she inherited, so far as the documents show, no blood of the negro." Yet, despite the lack of conclusive evidence, Markus asserts that Elizabeth Barrett "believed she had African blood through her grandfather Charles Moulton," who in 1782 had married the daughter of Edward Barrett of Cinnamon Hill, one of the wealthiest sugarcane planters in Jamaica.

Markus's tenuous claim is based on a statement written by Elizabeth Barrett in a letter to Robert Browning: "I would give ten towns in Norfolk (if I had them) to own some purer lineage than that of the blood of the slave! – Cursed we are from generation to generation!" This remark has customarily been considered an expression of regret that "the Barrett family fortune had been founded on the slave-worked sugar plantations of the West Indies," as glossed by Daniel Karlin in his 1989 edition of selections from the poets' correspondence and as assumed by Peter Dally in his *Elizabeth Barrett Browning: A Psychological Portrait* (1989).

But Markus interprets Elizabeth's declaration as an acknowledgment of her own "African blood," the crucial clue in the mystery of the Barrett family: "Why didn't Edward Barrett Moulton Barrett want his children to marry?" Although he fathered twelve children, he withheld permission for them to marry, and he disinherited those who married anyway, beginning with Elizabeth. Markus asks, "Was there, in her poor father's peculiar imagination and in his Christian conscience, the possibility that among his grandchildren he might someday be faced with one who was *not* of the slave master's race? Was he suffocating that dark-skinned grandchild by not allowing his children the slightest romantic interest?"

For once we have a plausible explanation of Edward Barrett's motives, in contrast to previous suppositions that he simply wished to control every aspect of his children's lives or that he wished to protect them from heartbreak at the death of a spouse or child. On the other hand, if he did not want his family line to continue, why father twelve children? Markus suggests, "He may have found out about the possibility of his mixed blood during the later years of his marriage, or it might have been that the issue of mixed blood was not a concern to the powerful heir to Cinnamon Hill during the years of prosperity. After all, such things were common in Creole families. But as his private fortunes declined, and the source of his wealth became anathema to the British people, he grew to believe he and his family were cursed, and he tried to control his children and to extinguish the possibility of a next generation. Who knows the mental sufferings of Edward Barrett Moulton Barrett in this area of legitimate procreation? Racist fears based on family secrets would certainly explain why the news of grandchildren did nothing to mollify his extreme position. A married child was a dead child. His grandchildren didn't exist for him."

Well, so what? We all have "mixed blood," and race is a false concept, as unreal as racism is real. Markus says that Elizabeth Barrett "was not proud of this lineage 'of the blood of the slave.' She was much too close to its ramifications, both in moral and in family matters. Yet in the high pitch of her creative intelligence and her nervous susceptibilities, she may have left the world a body of poetry that to some extent merged disparate cultures into a unique and increasingly radical voice." When an American magazine requested an abolitionist poem, she wrote on her honeymoon "The Runaway Slave at Pilgrim's Point," about a distraught slave who kills her child born after she has been raped by some members of "the Washington-race." With *Casa Guidi Windows* and *Poems before Congress,* Barrett Browning continued writing about oppression. She became the most impassioned and powerful political poet of the Victorian age, tremendously popular, although some reviewers chided her for naively addressing topics beyond the comprehension of women.

This from the most famous invalid in English poetry – and the strangest except for Eugene Lee-Hamilton. The nature of her malady remains unclear. The psychological portraitist Peter Dally deems her an agoraphobic and anorexic opium addict suffering from tuberculosis. Markus suspects bronchiectasis, not tuberculosis, which could have been accurately diagnosed at that time. Until she was fifteen, Elizabeth, the oldest of the Barrett children, had been quite active, roaming her family's five-hundred-acre estate in Herefordshire. Then in 1821 she fell seriously ill with a painful debilitation for which she took opium and morphine throughout the rest of her life. Moreover, she was deeply affected by the deaths of her nurturant mother in 1828, her grandmother Elizabeth in 1830, her uncle Samuel in 1837, her brother Samuel in 1840, and her favorite brother, Edward, nicknamed Bro, who drowned at Torquay in 1840 at the age of thirty-three. Because Bro had accompanied her there to help her convalesce, she was traumatized with a remorse as crushing as it was irrational. Hardly able to walk, she languished in the morbidity of her early poems.

When Robert Browning met her in her gloomy London sickroom in May 1845, after four months of intense correspondence, he believed that she had a spinal disease, and he probably assumed that sexual activity was out of the question. During their courtship, her health gradually improved, however, and in September 1846 they married secretly and scampered to Italy. She soon became pregnant, at the age of forty, and in the following four years survived four miscarriages. Their only child, a son born in 1849, became a painter and sculptor and died in 1912. Although they made occasional trips to England, Elizabeth never saw her father again, because of his refusal, and Robert never again saw his mother, who died suddenly in 1849. He was overcome with a remorseful grief, and it was then that Elizabeth showed him a manuscript she'd written during their courtship: the poems subsequently entitled *Sonnets from the Portuguese*, about their love, which had restored her to life.

Having delimited *Dared and Done* to the Brownings' marriage, Markus frog-marches the reader through the courtship, which has already been exhaustively indagated by Daniel Karlin in *The Courtship of Robert*

Browning and Elizabeth Barrett (1985), an antidote to the mawkish kitsch of Rudolf Besier's play *The Barretts of Wimpole Street* (1930). For a biography of the Brownings' son, see Maisie Ward's *The Tragi-Comedy of Pen Browning* (1972), and for a biography of Elizabeth's spaniel, see Virginia Woolf's *Flush* (1933). The poets' early years are recounted in John Maynard's *Browning's Youth* (1977) and Margaret Forster's *Elizabeth Barrett Browning: The Life and Loves of a Poet* (1988). Forster particularly illuminates the emotional machinations of the Barrett family and Elizabeth's close relationship with her favorite brother, Bro. Although sympathetic, Forster is not adulatory, especially in her revelations about Elizabeth's sometimes callous attitude toward her devoted maid, Elizabeth Wilson, whom Forster has made the heroine of her novel *Lady's Maid* (1990). In *Dared and Done*, Markus scants Wilson, touches on the Brownings' childhoods only in scattered flashbacks, and scorns old-fashioned chronological narrative, liberating her text from the bondage of time while manacling the inquisitive reader to the index and stumbling into clumsy repetitions. Another item for Ripley: believe it or not, Elizabeth Barrett and Robert Browning had only one child, yet he was born three times, on pages 130, 139, and 161.

Despite these shortcomings, *Dared and Done* has such notable long-goings as its compilation of rumors about African ancestry and descriptions of the Brownings' acquaintances: the painters and sculptors Benjamin Robert Haydon, Harriet Hosmer, William Page, Hiram Powers, and William Wetmore Story, one of Robert's closest friends, and the writers Isa Blagden, Margaret Fuller, Anna Jameson, Elizabeth Kinney, Walter Savage Landor, Edward Bulwer-Lytton, Robert Lytton, Mary Russell Mitford, John Ruskin, and Georges Sand, Elizabeth's haughty idol. Markus describes at length Elizabeth's involvement with the wealthy poet Sophia Eckley, who shared her enthusiasm for automatic writing and séances with rapping spirits and spectral hands, levitating tables and accordions played by phantoms, all to Robert's skeptical scorn. There's a book about that, too: Katherine H. Porter's *Through a Glass Darkly: Spiritualism in the Browning Circle* (1958). Though *Dared and Done* is not a critical biography, Markus delineates the personal sources of Browning's poems "Andrea del Sarto," "Bishop Blougram's Apology," "Mr. Sludge, 'The Medium,'" "One Word More," and *La Saisiaz*. And, having thoroughly annotated a 1977 edition of *Casa Guidi Windows*, about the Italian *risorgimento*, Markus is well qualified to explain the historical situation and the enduring significance of Barrett Browning's political poetry.

By the time she published her long poem *Casa Guidi Windows* in 1851, Elizabeth Barrett Browning had become a prominent poet, much more admired than her husband, whose poetry was often dismissed as willfully obscure. With such poems as "The Lost Bower" and "Hector in the Garden," she had become the finest poet of English gardens and fields since Andrew Marvell. Her "Lady Geraldine's Courtship" and "The Romance of the Swan's Nest" share the sensuosity of the works of Tennyson, Keats, and Pope. With her poems on the real difficulties of love, such as "A Denial" and "Confessions," transcending the strains of traditional amorous warblers, she rivals her husband and the younger poets George Meredith and Dante Gabriel Rossetti. And she strikes a Blakean chord with her songs of experience such as "The Cry of the Children," on working in coal mines and factories, and "Hiram Powers' Greek Slave," on the statue that can "strike and shame the strong, / By thunders of white silence."

In *Casa Guidi Windows*, she surpasses Restoration and Augustan satirists by evolving a partisan yet universal mode of political poetry that analyzes historic individuals defined by their actions and official roles. Thus Pope Pius IX, whom many pundits expected to lead Italy to unification and independence, is limited:

He's pope – we want a man! his heart beats warm,
  But, like the prince enchanted to the waist,
He sits in stone, and hardens by a charm
  Into the marble of his throne high-placed.

The first part of *Casa Guidi Windows* was originally entitled "Meditation in Tuscany," but it's an unusually dramatic meditation because Barrett Browning apostrophizes the Pope, Michelangelo, Dante, and Italian citizens in general, living and dead, and she supplies vehement speeches by Michelangelo, Savonarola, and other Florentines. In the second part, she praises such heroic freedom fighters as Anita Garibaldi and caustically laments the duplicity of ineffectual leaders, the vacillation of the public, and the hypocritical neutrality of countries such as "imperial England." In strophes of Sicilian sestets, shimmering between Dante's terza rima and Byron's ottava rima, she sounds a clarion challenge, while evoking Italy's hopeful past and glorious future.

Markus comments that although Italians honored her as a poet of the *risorgimento*, "English and American critics have not seriously considered Barrett Browning in this role. On the contrary, because of its political concerns, the poem has often been dismissed. Henry James understood the perceptivity of the poet's political point of view; he was closer to her time, but he felt that politics as a subject diminished her poetry. 'The cause of Italy was, obviously, for Mrs. Browning as high aloft as any object of interest could be; but that was only because she had let down, as it were, her inspiration and her poetic pitch.' Certainly this formalistic stance merged well with the ensuing New Criticism, and one can understand why a poem such as *Casa Guidi Windows* would be overlooked through the 1950s." But, Markus continues, "as the critics of the 1960s began to discover that a poem can both 'mean' and 'be,' and as political commitment began to be viewed as no anathema to artistic expression, one could have hoped for a reevaluation of Barrett Browning's Italian period. None was forthcoming."

Imperial England was not amused by *Casa Guidi Windows*, and sales were disappointing. In 1856, however, *Aurora Leigh* won immediate acclaim and remained in print for decades, until Barrett Browning was marginalized in a long Luciferian fall from critical grace, documented in Marjorie Stone's *Elizabeth Barrett Browning* (1995). But George Eliot praised *Aurora Leigh*, Ruskin raved, and Swinburne later wrote, "It is one of the longest poems in the world, and there is not a dead line in it."

Aurora Leigh is a first-person, blank-verse, cornucopiate *Künstlerroman* in which the eponymous orphan becomes a loveless though lionized poet. She rejects a marriage proposal from her wealthy cousin Romney Leigh, a social reformer who turns his ancestral hall into an ill-fated Fourierist phalanstery. He is kind, generous, altruistic, yet he teases Aurora for her poetic aspirations:

The human race
To you means, such a child, or such a man,
You saw one morning waiting in the cold,
Beside that gate, perhaps. You gather up
A few such cases, and when strong sometimes
Will write of factories and of slaves, as if
Your father were a negro, and your son
A spinner in the mills.

Romney runs into difficulties with the much abused but courageous seamstress Marian Erle and the cunning Lady Waldemar, who is limned with a labial luxuriance that would have made Keats blush:

The woman looked immortal. How they told,
Those alabaster shoulders and bare breasts,
On which the pearls, drowned out of sight in milk,
Were lost, excepting for the ruby-clasp!
They split the amaranth velvet bodice down

To the waist or nearly, with the audacious press
Of full-breathed beauty.

In dramatic scenes of varied cadences, now sedate, now exhilarated, Barrett Browning portrays the society of her time, of London, Paris, and Florence, city streets and country roads, salons of wit and hovels of billingsgate, class conflict and self-deprivation, meanwhile creating one of the few convincing fictitious poets in English literature. Along the way, Aurora Leigh develops a spiritual aesthetic of a Swedenborgian "double vision" of the "twofold world" of a suffering "prophet-poet" who

says the word so that it burns you through
With a special revelation, shakes the heart
Of all the men and women in the world,
As if one came back from the dead and spoke,
With eyes too happy, a familiar thing
Become divine i' the utterance! while for him
The poet, speaker, he expands with joy;
The palpitating angel in his flesh
Thrills inly with consenting fellowship
To those innumerous spirits who sun themselves
Outside of time.
O life, O poetry
– Which means life in life! cognisant of life
Beyond this blood-beat, passionate for truth
Beyond these senses!

And she anticipates both Yeats and Nabokov:

What is art
But life upon the larger scale, the higher,
When, graduating up in a spiral line
Of still expanding and ascending gyres,
It pushes toward the intense significance
Of all things, hungry for the Infinite?

In Florence in 1861, after fifteen years of marriage, at the age of fifty-five, Elizabeth died in Robert's arms, and although he lived another twenty-eight years, he never remarried. As his literary reputation grew, Browning became so bombastic that Henry James was puzzled that he could write poetry of such psychological nuance. In 1892 in his science-fiction tale "The Private Life" James transmogrified the late Robert Browning into a novelist called "Clare Vawdrey, the greatest (in the opinion of many) of our literary glories." The Jamesian narrator confides, "I never found him anything but loud and liberal and cheerful, and I never heard him utter a paradox or express a shade or play with an idea." In his conversation, he "disappoints every one who looks in him for the genius that created the pages they adore." Vawdrey, we eventually learn, has an "alternate identity," a ghostly "other self," a double who stays in his room and writes brilliantly in the dark while his crass self sallies forth into society to "gossip and dine by deputy."

As Lafcadio Hearn observes, Robert Browning "is especially the poet of character, the only one who has taught us, since Shakespeare's time, what real men and women are, how different each from every other, how unclassifiable according to any general rule, how differently noble at their best, how differently wicked at their worst, how altogether marvelous and infinitely interesting. His mission has been the mission of a great dramatic psychologist." Indeed, in his twenties, Browning wrote several unsuccessful plays, and he then settled on poetry but not fiction, oddly, since his verse often seems labored. The future poet laureate Alfred Austin remarked that Browning, like Molière's Monsieur Jourdain, wrote prose without realizing it. At times, however, Browning was inspired in meter and rhyme, as with "'Childe Roland to the Dark Tower Came,'" "My Last Duchess," and "Porphyria's Lover," but although he read widely, he lacked his wife's aesthetic response, as in *Aurora Leigh*:

when the rhythmic turbulence
Of blood and brain swept outward upon words,
As wind upon the alders, blanching them
By turning up their under-natures till
They trembled in dilation.

Her extraordinary talent attracted Edgar Allan Poe, who dedicated *The Raven and Other Poems* to her, although they never met. In his 1845 review of *A Drama of Exile and Other Poems*, Poe catalogues her many "foibles" of construction, imagery, and versification, including slant rhyme and irregular rhythm. "The Cry of the Children," for example, "cannot be scanned: we never saw so poor a specimen of verse," yet that poem "is full of a nervous unflinching energy – a horror sublime in its simplicity – of which Dante himself might have been proud." Of her line "Shining eyes, like antique jewels set in Parian statue-stone," Poe prophesies that "from the entire range of poetical literature there shall not, in a century, be produced a more sonorous – a more vigorous verse – a juster – a nobler - a more ideal – a more magnificent image." Nevertheless, her poetry achieves no "sustained effort": "Her wild and magnificent genius seems to have contented itself with points – to have exhausted itself in flashes; but it is the profusion – the unparalleled number and close propinquity of these points and flashes which render her book *one flame*, and justify us in calling her unhesitatingly, the greatest – the most glorious of her sex." And, furthermore, "she has surpassed all her poetical contemporaries of either sex (with a single exception)." The exception is Tennyson, yet she has "an imagination even more vigorous than his."

Alas, Poe died years before the appearance of *Aurora Leigh* and Barrett Browning's delirious "Bianca among the Nightingales." Wonderment at what supernal ecstasy of rhythmic turbulence might have swept through his weird brain renders one speechless.

JONATHAN SISSON

REWARDS AND TRANSFORMATIONS

Middens of the Tribe, poems by Daniel Hoffman (Louisiana State University Press, 77 pp., Baton Rouge, 1995; hardback, $17.95; paper, $9.95).
The Country of the Blue, poems by Charles Edward Eaton (Cornwall Books, 110 pp., New York, 1994; hardback, $16.95).
Crazy Horse In Stillness, poems by William Heyen (BOA Editions, Ltd., 271 pp., Brockport, NY, 1996; paper, $15).

These three established poets (the youngest, Heyen, was born in 1940), have made indelible marks on the contemporary poetry scene, and each of these works definitively illustrates these poets' considerable gifts.

Though the Russian scholar Bakhtin emphasized fiction when illustrating his dialogic theory, Daniel Hoffman's *Middens of the Tribe* delivers a succession of interrelated poems as a compendium of multiple voices working harmoniously. In this compelling page-turner (not be taken pejoratively), Hoffman concocts plot and subplot involving an aging businessman, his son who's taken over the company, and their mistresses. Numerous characters speak either through dramatic monologue, reflective first person, or omniscient third person. An impersonal voice occasionally interrupts the characters with information regarding cultural practices of the Cromlech People that mirror the contemporary characters' situations: "We find no evidence of adolescent / rebellion against the ascription of fixed / roles." When this voice asks where the Cromlechs "purge. . . those anarchic energies," he hypothesizes, "upon their funeral urns, their buried flutes, looked to the walls of their caves." In the following poem, a painter struggles with giving up "literal depiction" of his model for "the power of Woman, the immortal energy / that called from him this glimpse of pure emotion."

While suspension of certain pieces of the plot's puzzle adds to narrative tension, Hoffman's use of pronouns in place of proper names can be needlessly frustrating. Poem (chapter?) 11 begins "He has no daughter," and nowhere in the three-page poem is the man named, though eventually the reader recognizes a central character in flashback. Perhaps Hoffman's intent is to have the reader put the puzzle together just as the overseeing persona attempts to do in stalking his ancestral scraps (the middens – literally scraps of garbage – of his tribe) for a family history that delivers a modicum of sense, that puts form to formlessness.

Water appears in all of Charles Edward Eaton's poems in his aptly-titled book, *The Country of the Blue*. This is sensual – and sensuous – verse. Not since e.e. cummings has any writer delivered so many original erotic and tender love poems that convince with such startling details. On board "The River Boat" the lovers' "little portable cranked out love songs," and "If the universe moves too forcefully, / Even a glancing kiss rips off its skin." An allusion to Cleopatra's barge appears in more than one poem, an appropriate metaphor for the whole book, the slow weight of the poems' lives, pentameters or longer, floats the reader mellifluously along.

A few poems will highlight the whole. "Periscope" puns with submarine diction to describe lovemaking: "You lay with her in a wash of flowers, / This roll in her soft arms of a beached thing, / Back and forth still so heavy with pressure." The book's final poem, "The Cove," juxtaposing three schools of images – boating, writing, and love-making – begins, "His boat had lost its calligraphic power, / The placid water like a vast blue mirror / That swallowed all his spoken sentences." Toward the end, "I feel the topaz leaching from my arms, / And I study all my old incisions. / If she could read me like a book, it would / Be lurid with just this love of living." Eaton's poetry delights us with such word play. "Luxuriant blue tatoos from the warm water / As if the sun were needling you again" comically connect the vernacular with the formal, the natural with the artificial.

The final book under review, William Heyen's *Crazy Horse in Stillness*, focuses on the two leaders of the Battle of Little Big Horn, Custer and Crazy Horse. Though the general movement of the short poems' clustering is chronological, a non-linear emphasis in most verses deconstructs cause-and-event history. In the Afterword, Heyen reveals that the poems "were written by way of their sounds and their flow/cut/plunge from line to line, & not by way, of course, of argument or idea." The poems hopefully will induce, he continues, a visionary experience close to the "states of reverie" he experienced as a child and led him to believe he "lived the life. . . .that the Lakota boy, who was born a century before I was and who would later receive the name Crazy Horse, lived."

The character of General George Custer represents the white man's rational, positivistic mind, and Crazy Horse the Native American's natural, ecological point of view. Both emerge as individuals. As a child, Crazy Horse sits "in a pit covered with branches. . . . / his own wings spread," while Custer grouses about getting "some god-damned decent chow beyond this West Point / chipped prairie dog shit / on toast." Crazy Horse enters a trance in which words turn sacred, "the Great Mystery of the single word of being," while "Plebe Custer perused his grammar text. . . . / the subject being (him)self, & understood." Years later, Crazy Horse metamorphoses into nature: "More than once, he'd been an animal, but / which? – *buffalo* or *bear*," while Custer writes to his wife, "I have a fine buffalo head for you."

But the book's most extraordinary vision arrives after the battle of Little Big Horn when the men, both dead, meet in a series of anachronistic poems: "The two sat under a willow near a river, / facing one another. I wanted to tell you, said Custer: like all the rest, my employer / is down-sizing." Later,

Crazy Horse, Custer, & the white buffalo sat down to
  talk,
but the buffalo said nothing. Crazy Horse also said
  nothing, as, in good faith, Custer rambled on,
his head filled with churches whose steeples
impaled the Indians & the heads.

Custer remains alienated from nature even in death. When Crazy Horse encounters a shopping mall's grand opening, he avoids its appeal: "He will visit that place, / but not today. Today, herds still migrate / beyond the shafts of acetylene light." The buffalo remains Crazy Horse's symbolic and literal refuge, as prefigured in the book's first poem: "*my nose buried in its fur I sleep / its fur wet it smells of dung & grass*." The absence of punctuation reinforces the Lakota boy's connectedness to the animal, the fusing of consciousness complete.

All three books deliver rewards, and I look forward to revisiting each. They are certain to elicit admiration in all readers, and also, perhaps, for some, transformation.

RICHARD HOLINGER

TWO MEMOIRS, ONE JOURNAL

The Liar's Club, by Mary Karr (Viking Press, New York, 1995, 320 pp.; cloth, $22.95;$12.95, paper).
Writing Was Everything, by Alfred Kazin (Harvard University Press, Cambridge, MA 02138, 1995, 152 pp.; cloth, $17.95).
A Lifetime Burning In Every Moment: From the Journals of Alfred Kazin (Harper Collins, New York, 1996, 341 pp.; cloth, $26).

One of the first things a reader is bound to notice about Mary Karr's memoir, *The Liar's Club*, is how salty the language is. But so what? you say. The story is set in deep East Texas, and isn't that the way "those people" talk? Well, yes and no. Some of us (I speak as a native East Texan now), once we've managed to get away and pick up a little schooling, are actually able to express ourselves from time to time with words that don't involve body functions. In her book, Karr writes from the point of view of a mature woman looking back on a time when she was a little girl in a troubled family. But the mature Karr, who is well into middle age now, attended both Macalester and Goddard Colleges and now teaches literature and creative writing at Syracuse University, after having also taught at Tufts, Harvard and Sarah Lawrence. In addition, she's an ambitious poet, with three collections to her credit. So the question arises, whose voice is this? It's a grating, mock-tough voice, not at all like the voice found in Karr's poetry, and one has to wonder if maybe it isn't some New York editor's or agent's idea of what a book set in East Texas *ought* to sound like. (I've been told by someone who knows Mary Karr that she really does talk that way, even today, but what it says about her, if true, is too dreary to contemplate.)

The events depicted in *The Liar's Club* are taken for the most part from just two years in the author's life: 1962, when she was seven and living with her family in "Leechfield," a fictionalized oil town down near the Texas Gulf Coast, and 1963, when she and her older sister Lecia are living with her mother and her mother's new boyfriend Hector in a small town in Colorado. Mary, or "Pokey" as her father fondly calls her, is sexually abused in both states. In Texas, it's by a teenage boy, who rapes her, and in Colorado it's by a male babysitter, who forces here to perform fellatio on him. Both scenes are powerful and well rendered.

But the core of the book is not Pokey; it's her parents, especially her mother, Charlie Mae, a restless, unhappy housewife. Pokey has a low opinion of her mother. In marrying Pete Karr, a refinery worker, Charlie Mae feels she has demeaned herself. She had lived briefly in New York City during an earlier, ill-fated marriage and has come away from the experience with intellectual and artistic pretensions. She reads Sartre and Camus. She's a would-be painter. *Anna Karenina*, we're told, is her favorite novel. She also drinks a lot and takes a lot of pills. In a word, she's "nervous", which as Karr says is an East Texas locution covering everything from nail-biting to full-blown psychosis. She also carries around with her a guilty secret which won't be revealed to the reader until the book's somewhat stagey climax.

Pete Karr, on the other hand, is the salt of the earth. The narrator adores him. He may be rough-hewn but he's got a heart as big as Texas. He was a hero in World War Two and has the shrapnel wound to prove it. He also spins a mean anecdote, usually of the tall-tale variety, when he's among his card-playing buddies down at the American Legion hall, thus accounting for the book's title. When Charlie Mae sends Pete packing shortly after the family's arrival in Colorado, an already dark narrative suddenly turns much darker. Booze, pills, promiscuity and eventually madness become even more the order of the day.

"Without him," Karr laments in the wake of her father's departure, "Mother's misery was seeping in. Happiness was for boneheads, a dumb fog you sank into. Pain, low-level and constant, was a vigil you kept."

The picture Karr paints of her mother is not a pretty one. And the revelations contained in the book's final chapter do not in any way absolve her, as they seem meant to do, of the sluttishness and general all-around bad behavior she exhibits throughout the rest of the book. Her treatment of her husband alone is enough to brand her as a monster, and the self-centered carelessness with which this parent of two small daughters squanders a small fortune bequeathed to her by her own dying mother almost defies belief. All of this is extremely poignant when, checking the acknowledgments page, we see that the author has thanked her for her "support" in the book's writing.

Writing Was Everything, Alfred Kazin's first book under review here, is a memoir of another sort. There's very little of the personal in it. It's mostly a record of one man's peregrinations in the world of New York literary criticism. Kazin discusses mentors and friends and offers up an array of opinions about authors he knew and books he read. This little volume began as one of the Massey Lectures in the History of American Civilization delivered each year at Harvard – in this case, 1994 – and with its broad strokes and rhetorical flourishes, it reads like something that might have been spoken aloud in an auditorium.

Two of the writers who attract much of Kazin's attention are that seemingly disparate pair, John Cheever and Franz Kafka. Kazin died of prostate cancer on his 83rd birthday in June 1998. In this short book, he talks of meeting Cheever when he and the late novelist and short story writer were both very young men, haunting the "hunger bench" outside the editorial offices of *The New Republic* in hopes of picking up free-lance reviewing assignments. Cheever's later prose style was marred by being forced into *The New Yorker* magazine's rigid mold, Kazin feels. "Still the stories were wryly serious, desperately ironic, full of that special distrust of postwar American hedonism felt to the point of hysteria by those who had seen the depression end, but only with the war," writes Kazin. "And they were funny, in Cheever's politely macabre way, with the contrast between suburbia and the despair within, which sounded like a kind of mutiny against family life that could not hope to succeed."

Regarding Kafka, Kazin mentions the critical controversy surrounding the Czech writer's work in the wake of World War Two and the Holocaust, with Harold Rosenberg, for instance, championing it and Edmund Wilson damning it as worthless. Then he quotes the art collector Bernard Berenson as having "severely warned" him (Kazin) in Rome in 1947 that "'There is a very small light of reason burning in the world. Mr. Kafka is trying to put it out.'"

In his own lumpily eloquent defense of Kafka, Kazin remarks: "The mind can describe many processes in nature, but soon or later the mind, despite what science boasts, cannot be satisfactorily correlated with all that exists outside it. This is the abyss literature fills, though never so fully that we cannot still hear the wailing of Job and Lear."

A Lifetime Burning in Every Moment turns out to be a single-volume selection of excerpts from journals Kazin kept for more than fifty years. Here we see Kazin responding to the world around him, more or less as he found it at the time. Some of these journal entries seem less than spontaneous, however, and appear more than a little tailored to a day when they might be fitted between the covers of just such as book as this.

They begin in the heady days before World War Two, when large events are converging and changing the very atmosphere of the author's New York literary world. Fascism is on the rise. Will Kazin and his friends on the socialist left be able to stop it? This period and the immediate post-war era of Germany's defeat, the discovery of the Holocaust, and American triumphalism make up roughly half the volume – and provide its most interesting entries. The personal observations are sharper here, the reportorial eye and interviewing skills more keenly honed.

Here, for example, is Kazin describing his impressions of T. S. Eliot after a 1945 interview in the poet's office at Faber and Faber in London: "Looks like a very sensitive question mark – long, winding, and bent. Gives the impression that his sensibility is in his long, curling nose and astonishing hands.

I was afraid he would be standoffish and nervously yammered on, but to my relief he kept bringing the conversation back to America. . . . To my astonishment, he asked, 'By the way, what's this Truman like?' In the nick of time, I replied, 'You ought to know. You both come from Missouri.'"

And here Kazin is, again, on Bernard Berenson, in this same post-war period: "He spoke English with such severe and careful diction, delivering himself formally of his words, one by one, that he might have been putting freshly cracked walnuts into my hand. What a superior act he puts on."

But this freshness, these sharply etched little vignettes of personal observation, give way in the second half of the book to a pervasive gloominess and sour introspection that make for much less enjoyable reading. It's clear that Kazin's last years were not particularly happy. His several divorces are recounted and a sense of swelling resentment and bitterness begin to emerge. American literary culture didn't turn out the way the brash young critic of the '30s had thought it would. None of the old verities are honored anymore. His journal entries become petulant, even nasty at times, as when he describes the piggishness with which A. J. Liebling had just devoured a meal in his presence. Also, Kazin's old friends, Irving Kristol and Saul Bellow, have become, in his view, right-wingers, and this seems to leave him utterly at a loss. Then, Kazin's preoccupations with Jews and Jewishness, present throughout the book, becomes much more pronounced in the second half. Entry after entry is devoted to the subject. This is understandable, in part, as one Jew's reaction to the enormity of the Holocaust, but some of the stuff is so intramural that after a while a non-Jewish reader begins to feel like an eavesdropper.

By the time he reached the 1990s, Kazin was totally disenchanted with the world that confronted him every day. Here's part of a typical journal entry: ". . . . What sickens me in 1993, as it could never have done in the terrible 1933, though Hitler was in power and we were mired in a depression that lifted only with the war, is how limited everyone seems to me – myself not least, how transparent every motive. People have never before seemed to me so narrow and irremediable. The language almost everyone talks around me comes straight out of a TV commercial. . . . It is as boring to list everything I hate as it is to live with this hatefulness. . . . "

The abyss, it was clear, grew ever nearer and – for Kazin – literature no longer filled it.

ROBERT LACY

FOUR BOOKS OF POEMS

Aimless Life Poems 1961-1995, by George T. Wright (North Stone Editions, Box 14098, Minneapolis, MN 55414-0098, 1999, 222 pp.; hardback, $35; paper, $15).

What Do I Know? New & Selected Poems, by John Calvin Rezmerski (Holy Cow Press, Box 3170, Mount Royal Station, Duluth, MN 55803, 2000, 134 pp.; paper, $13.95).

The Dark Indigo Current, poems by Thomas R. Smith (Holy Cow Press, Box 3170, Mount Royal Station, Duluth, MN 55803, 2000, 79 pp.; $12.95, paper).

Temporary Help, poems by John Engman (edited by John Mitchell; Holy Cow Press, Box 3170, Mount Royal Station, Duluth, MN 55803, 1998, 105 pp,; $12.95, paper).

A Navajo wind chant tells us that it is important to "remember what you have seen because everything forgotten returns to the circling winds." For each of these books, the author demonstrates in his own distinctive voice the ways and means of remembering; it is a re-naming which enables the poet to understand and embrace more freely the mysteries of time and loss. When we remember, we are no longer victims of what time and events have wrought. When we remember, we are able to reclaim and repossess those events in time so that we do not become possessed.

Aimless Life, George T. Wright's collection, evokes memories and dreams shadowed by a lingering regret for being one of the last survivors, yet always mindful of those who have gone before and who have molded the inner life. In the prologue, "Late Letter to My Father" acknowledges the deep influence his father had on the poet: "As I grow older, / I have adopted you." This adoption is difficult to admit since it comes with the continuous awareness of that inherited rootlessness which inspires wanderings, "our common drift":

> Now that I work it through,
> this way we have
> of abandoning every position
> without strict loss
> to keep some central composure,
> this weakness for chronic exile
> disguised as settling,
> is shared more widely than we think:
> not wholly shameful,

not continually rankling,
but a foraging outward to find
what abides in crisis.

The poet more often than not becomes the carrier or caretaker of memories such as in "Spring" when ". . .Time, / That gave me verdue once, now leaves me rime." Ultimately the saving grace of lost time becomes the poet's profession which allows the sensual delights of spring to seep into the bone like warm air: "Four butterflies askew across the yard / Fly through the moment into my poem and / Are swallowed by existence like a sword. / To keep the springtime steady to my hand, / I need a sacred song, a prosperous wand." And it is this "sacred song" by which the poet prospers. In "Weekend in the Smokies," that same salvation which the creative spirit offers is requested by the poet once again: "For only a moment, not used to waiting, I wait, / I wait with the hills – then, restless, ask that breeze, that caw, / that edge of sun on the far slope lighting its green, / tree by tree, not questions only but favors: / *How does the drying blood within me join us? / What river are we? Take place in my poem.*" This humble quest for these favors permits the poet to partake – briefly yet deeply – in the mysteries; it is a balm for the poet which heals.

It is not only writing which lets the poet live close to the flame of the creative spirit, but the very process of reading, discovering and sharing worlds and words – that time-worn yet wondrous language of poetry – which sets us free: "after a while the lives about me make / a wall of flames against which, scorched and laddered, / I lean, and haul my fire-life, and climb. // The whole sky crackles as I read my book." ("Fire-Life") Essentially, by partaking of the process of reading and studying, the poet suggests that "this is the way I learn, love, flare, grow old. / Yea, though I sleep, though dark hours, days, dim me, / my house is eaten through and through with light." The reader, as well, is a captive audience in this wondrous house of light.

A beautiful mixture of rhyme and blank verse laced with an intricate inner rhythm is exhibited in "Nocturne." Here Wright captures the very pulse of night, as if the reader were right there listening to the very sounds and crickets and trains that haunt the night. The poet teaches us how to listen:

Now night uncloses
its box of far noises
and sets them out for each
waker, worker, or even
the long breather, whose vaults, love,

> lie open
> to forms of the waves' subsiding,
> chords of the cricket's
> bow, the bruised sound
> of that train in the distance,
> or here at hand, near,
> the breeze riffling trees.
> *What do we mean?* they all
> ask as they measure
> night for their listeners.

Wright is a poet's poet and if we were to listen well to his voice we would be enlightened and inspired by the beautiful, beguiling music which if read with heart and mind gives one a renewed appreciation of the power and meaning of poetry.

What Do I Know? by John Calvin Rezmerski reinforces the poet's introductory statement that "a poem is not an artifact to be preserved in a library like a museum exhibit, but an act of communication in which readers need to be consulted." This act of communication asks the reader with a gentle, koan-like question which more often than not can never be answered completely or finally: "What do I know?" Just as well, this question can be synonymous with that eternally asked "Who am I? Who are you?" As Rezmerski admits, "the question does not demand a single answer, but requires a list, a catalog, a request for suggestions, as well as changes of mind." So the poet here dons his multifaceted hat of many colors and is adept at humor, narrative prose, and lyrical rhapsodies. However, Rezmerski utilizes to the fullest extent the power of poetry's oral tradition fulfilling Marianne Moore's definition of poetry ("an imaginary garden with real toads in it"), while the reader, fallen under the poet's spell-binding auditory imagination, can hear in each fragile shell-like poem, the sound of the sea.

What Do I Know? is a collection (from 1969 to 1998) of new and previously published and unpublished poems. There is a Zen-inspired understanding evolving in many of Rezmerski's poems. In "Genesis," we are reminded not to "chide the children, / they are remembering things before they happen." In "Visit," a peeled orange becomes in an instant "a world / my eyes fly around." The poet in "Fall Morning" sees passing trucks become ships "standing in the fog, alone, / nobody has to believe me." The magic of Rezmerski's poetry is that we are inspired to believe him and, when he tells us in "Grandmother" that "in her house I learned to listen to seashells," we are allowed as well to listen and witness the evolution of his grandmother who "gives birth to the spirit / she has carried full term," while all along "the family closes around her / like a flower closing for the night." In "Way Back," the poet asks us to "turn around and come with me / to the other end of our lives" where we "begin / living backwards. / Moving toward my birth, / remembering less and less about death, / forgetting how to forget." It is a luminous understanding which enables us to become "equal to anyone – / a drop of slippery water / in a velvet sack." "Your Voice, October on the River" is a beautiful exegesis on the mysteries which exist between two people and how at certain times in one's life you are changed by that relationship which grows like a rose flower all around you: "you told me to watch how / the light fell yellow from the trees / in beads and drizzles – / so many different sunlights! / Falling as though the syllables of your voice / had come visible!"

The poet's journey into the power and magical intoxication of language culminates in his prose poems; there he allows his love of sound and the emotive nature of words to carry him (and us) away. In this journey we discover the paradoxical conundrum of the poet who enters into an experience which is essentially inarticulate, beyond the boundaries of words. It is for the poet to capture the meaning those inarticulate moments convey and try to translate their transforming and liberating message as benediction. In "Chin Music," the poet likes "to hear words gurgling over my teeth like orange pop, and to hear meanings going every whichway . . ." "A Little Chin Fugue for J. S. Bach" beautifully illustrates the multi-layered fluidity of words positioned in such a way as to be able to read them left to right, top to bottom or vice-versa. This poem is a fugue in itself which resonates after reading it again and again. "Sea Chanty" captures, as well, that beautiful fluidity of language which transports the reader to another place. These poems need to be read out loud like a chant or a mantra, for only then can they be internalized. Finally, "Morning on the Prairie" is a pure distillation of an exotic moment in the middle of nowhere which magically becomes everywhere: "And I was standing on the prairie near a river facing the sunrise, and all around me the ground was alive with crickets . . . a long way behind me I heard the hissing of the wind in the grass, and the hum of the sun warming the flies and bees, and the far-off groaning of the mountains shifting and the pounding of the oceans on both coasts in rhythm and under all the varied rhythms was one throb as though the continent were a person dancing, fingers snapping, hands clapping, teeth clacking, throat howling, and under it all the heart beat." John Calvin Rezmerski transposes his moment and by this transposition allows us once again to listen with him to the sound of the sea.

Thomas R. Smith's *The Dark Indigo Current* is not a comforting collection of poems for it is heavy with the burden of partings and farewells. At the heart of this book is a sequence of poems about the death of the poet's father. A. R. Ammons says "when a father dies / the sky becomes unlooped / from the stars." It is an emptiness that can never be filled. Perhaps it is in this very process of creativity whereby the poet is afforded the opportunity to heal that empty space, that renting hole. These poems try to bridge the gap between the living and the dead with the tenderness of memory and the forgiveness of love.

Many times the poet compares the process of dying to a mariner's journey across a vast, uncharted sea. In "Seafarers," Smith says "we are seafarers – we do not belong / to land. Shipwrecked is our destiny." In the sequence of poems about the death of his father, Smith glances back after viewing his father in the coffin and sees "the traveler floating in his open boat." (4. "Family Viewing") And at the graveside the poet lost in reverie reveals: "Here where your great-grandfather's / monument like an old ship captain // steers this crew of the dead among the carved / waves, we give you back to the corn – // fields and birches, and to that headstrong / river that tumulted through your life." (5. "The Burial") Our lives are "that dark indigo current" which rushes onward toward the unknown sea; and we, too, change into something rich and strange while death is near.

Often we are caught in our own mid-life journey, strangled by beginnings and ends simultaneously; children grow up and leave, parents grow old and die. We are filled with those empty spots of longing that do not save us, but Smith admits: "it's right to give our longing to the ocean – / and if someone speaks to us, that's a gift." ("Seafarer") There are many people who have touched us and who have spoken to us; even in death their lives are a gift with which we are continually blessed. In "Clearing a Woodyard," the spirit of the poet's grandfather seems to hover nearby: "I feel him closer in these vigorous / chores in sun and wind, as if that's / where he knows best how to return." And in those meditative times we are flooded with the forgiveness of remembering those we have loved and who have loved us: "but now / the old antagonisms drop away / and I'm flooded again with the power of loving him." ("Admiring My Father")

"Daffodils for Aunt Vic" is a memorable poem about being touched by those we love; even dying cannot change this. "I study your hands, so open from habit, a purse wrinkled with all // its giving, and think of the brushwood in Boncho's haiku, that goes on budding, // though cut." Like a dream re-entered or re-invented in order to experience our past, new revelations come to us that we are really not alone and death is not an end but a beginning. This is the time, then, as in "Housewarming," to forgive and be forgiven: "On Christmas Eve, I prepare a warm / place for my mother and father, sister / and brothers, grandparents, all my relatives / none dead, none missing, none angry / with another, all coming through the wood."

The Dark Indigo Current is an uncompromisingly truthful collection of poems that addresses the painful process of losing loved ones. In "The Reply," the poet asks "*what good have these poems done?*" One is reminded of Boncho's brushwood which buds even after it has been cut for the fire – so, too, these poems are a mirror image of that brushwood. Thomas R. Smith's poems bloom perfectly and continue to grace us with their mysterious, hard-won presences, their scent and beauty lingering in the reader's memory.

John Engman's *Temporary Help* is a posthumously published collection of poems which demonstrates what his literary predecessor Wallace Stevens has said a poet's subject should be – "his sense of the world." The book is deftly edited by John Mitchell, Engman's close friend and a professor at Augsburg College. Here we see that Engman's "sense of the world" motivates this eclectic range of poems, modulating from benign descriptions of urban living to a more malignant awareness of those frustrations which plague so many people trapped in a job that corrodes creative energies. There are also poems which address the vagaries of the human heart – seemingly so elusive to capture or control. However, *Temporary Help* is predominantly a book of poems which transcribes emotional and social alienation; inevitably, we are solitary, somewhat sad creatures, Engman attests ("and all this aloneness, my fame, like a leaf in stone"). Within this framework, however, Engman overlays a tapestry of images and words which transcends that alienation and aloneness and which ultimately saves us, changes us. Though he professes to be a "sad astronaut," his poetic vision is never denied or ignored, no matter if he has to "approach the moon on foot." Ultimately, we come to realize through Engman's poetry that it is the journey itself which is important, not the destination.

Temporary Help can be divided into three categories: poems about urban life, poems about love, and poems about self-awareness. Within each category, however, as within each poem, there is an image or symbol which allows the poet a brief glimpse into the nature of reality – his true sense of the world. It is a transcendent symbol which saves the poet/persona from alienation, depression, and ultimately death.

The poems centered upon urban life detail a close and intimate knowledge of neighbor's lives through those paper-thin apartment walls; however, it is an intimacy which is never initiated nor rebuked. Through all the crazy chaos of apartment living, the poet in "Creation of the Universe" sits "at my desk, as usual, writing a poem / as if working a puzzle, working a psalm." In "Gladioli," that psalm becomes a hymn as the poet sings to his "gladioli in a furnished room" while "you feel more alone than before, / feel your love for the whole world coming on // stronger than before . . . It isn't that you could love // everyone on earth with your small mind, but you do . . . Millions of years of human evolution and you are still / you: sad astronaut, approaching the moon on foot."

"Terrible Weather Conditions" is a poignant love poem which has no real resolution, but hangs heavily in the air like a blossom too full on a green stem, like a question unanswered: "Loud sky, red rain, white crow, moon flying away. How can I love you in autumn when everything goes wrong? / Last night, I burned three hundred calories dreaming about your hair. / I thought I felt animal earth lurch forward // and fell into the dark ages between now and now." This poem is a personal supplication which addresses the beloved and reader alike and asks if perhaps after all there could be permanence amid the chaos of impermanence, changelessness of love in a mutable, lonely world: "Someday, what will I be when I am nothing but a flutter behind your breastbone like a leaf falling? Will you be the sky?"

Many of Engman's poems have a cinematic quality – as if the perspective of the poet, beginning from far above, suddenly swoops down like a bird through the window to give us a closer look, a different perspective. Surprisingly, the persona of many of these cinematic poems seems to be caught off guard by what is seen, by what is revealed. In "A Bird Flies into the Room and Then Flies Out Again," the poet is saved from falling into self-pity by a simple yet remarkable event – a bird flying into a room; the open window becomes a symbol of the poet's receptivity to the world and the internal changes this receptivity can bring: "So I'm standing here in my winter underwear / and my room feels cold but suddenly good – / if this is the way the world ends, that's okay, / it's winter, and my window is wide open."

In the title poem, "Temporary Help," the day starts out with a sense of impending doom: "Today, I feel like the spirit children / of Atlantis prayed to, father of ghosts." The poem ends with a quiet benediction inspired by something as simple as a floating red balloon which the poet grasps, allowing him a moment of grace: "Still, something / a red balloon can bring against the gloom / seems really true, floating from nowhere / to the roof of a bus shelter. / I jump for the string." The red balloon becomes another transcendent symbol which liberates the poet from depression. It is a moment of grace which changes the poet forever: "These moments that could change me / forever don't come often enough / and when they come I don't often see, / although I remain alert and curious / as I work at my desk this morning, / this moment at the end of a century, / this hole in the day through which I fall / with earth as it falls through the sky, / the current universe before my eyes."

"Think of Me in D Major" (a winner of the Helen Bullis Prize) has that eerily translucent quality of premonitions fulfilled – one of Engman's best poems. The poem begins with a complaint of sorts about ill health and the attention of death behind all things: "I'm waiting for a doctor to check my pulse / and draw blood. I feel sick, not dying, / but scared, // and poor Johann Sebastian Bach is trying / to comfort me / in D Major." The poet admits "it's hard to believe that anyone can live / hopefully // if the body is simply a score written in red / and white counts, / brainwaves, x-rays." And, as if he is arguing with himself, the poet goes on to explain that it is "harder to believe that anyone can die / when Johann Sebastian Bach argues / for the soul // in D Major, a symphony of goosebumps. / Maybe what dying / organisms call / living is learning how to be swept away?" The poem concludes with a simple declaration of faith in the fullness of life after life, a powerful symbol of the spirit's rejuvenation: "So, if someday / I disappear, / just think of me as a goosebump, or a note / that disappears in D Major, swept away, / but still here."

After I finished this collection, John Engman's use of imaginative imagery and reverberating symbols, though etched (like his short life) "like a leaf in stone," changed my perceptions of both life and language, the highest compliment between poet and reader.

MARJORIE BUETTNER

EMILY CARTER'S STORIES

Glory Goes and Gets Some: Stories, by Emily Carter (Coffee House Press, 27 North Fourth Street, Suite 400, Minneapolis, MN 55401, 2000, 237 pages; hardback, $20.95).

I have a problem with much of today's autobiographical, confessional fiction. In many ways it seems beset with narcissistic monotony in the manner of conceptual art and performance art, with sordid themes of childhood and sexual abuse, substance and sex additions, therapy, HIV and AIDS. Because these themes have grown tiresome, I am a bit surprised that they continue to have cachet with art and publishing power brokers.

However that may be, I found Emily Carter's 21 interlinked stories artfully rendered, mostly in the voice of Gloria (Glory) Bronski, the gritty central character and alter ego of the author. Like Glory, Emily Carter is a recovering heroin addict who contracted HIV positive probably from an infected needle. Glory became HIV positive through an affair with a Puerto Rican air-conditioner repairman.

While the stories chronicle Glory's descent from the privileged daughter of upper-class Manhattan intellectuals to a homeless drug addict who trades sex for drugs, Carter doesn't wallow in self-pity. Instead, there is an uplifting quality to these sardonic pieces. This Glory is not a Victim. She's made her life choices and accepts them. Along the way she makes wry and often amusing observations. Glory skewers the silly psychobabble of therapists and clients in recovery programs. For instance, here is her take on Sherman Oates, the counselor in the story "A": "I wanted to call him Dr. Oates or Mr. Oates but he insisted on Sherman. When he said 'Sherman' as if we were friends, I felt that same sense of a hand being suddenly thrust up my skirt I'd felt in a thousand therapists' offices since I was three years old. He wore cable-knit sweaters, oatmeal-colored slacks of unbleached cotton, and his office was decorated with Native American artifacts. A copy of *Iron John* was casually tossed atop the clutter of an antique steamer trunk that served as a coffee table . . . Stephen seemed desperate, and God knows I'd been at the point where I'd clutched at homilies tossed out by every kind of New Age nutcake you could possibly imagine . . . 'We've been exploring Stephen's warrior spirit,' Sherman said . . . 'We've been talking about how it was his warrior spirit that has all but conquered the virus and restored him to physical health.' "

Recovery is the theme of these stories – recovery of Glory who has no need of self-discovery. She knows she's a drug addict looking for love. In the story "The Bride" Glory says that men have always had a power over her: ". . . even more than your average P.W.V., which stands for Person With A Vagina, the first of many acronyms in an initial-cluttered life . . . .From nursery school on, I craved their love and approval in the way I would later come to crave alcohol, cocaine, and opiates. 'Glory,' said my mother, 'is going to grow up to be a lover of men.' "

The Glory in these stories – like, I assume, her creator – is much more than that. She has lived a fascinating life well outside the mainstream. I am, however, curious about her next work, reportedly a novel. Emily Carter has already written her life. Will a work hewn from her imagination approach the potency of these fine stories?

MICHAEL FEDO

ON MICHAEL DENNIS BROWNE

Selected Poems: 1965-1995, by Michael Dennis Browne (Carnegie Mellon, 1997, 123 pp.; $11.95, paper).

The appearance of Michael Dennis Browne's fifth full collection of poems gives one sufficient pause to reflect on the output of his career. Browne's entry into the lists of American poets (although he was born and educated through his undergraduate years in England) came in the mid-1960s when he began publishing poems in *The New Yorker* while still a graduate student at the University of Iowa. The director of the Iowa Writers Workshop, George Starbuck, was so impressed by this that upon graduating from Iowa with a straight M.A. degree in English in 1967, Browne was offered a Visiting Lectureship at the Workshop, which meant that he would now teach graduate students from whose ranks he had just been elevated.

One of his early students, Darrell Gray (1945-1986), remarked later that Browne as a teacher emphasized "rhythm and music" in poems as being the most significant factors in distinguishing a good or even great poem from the mediocre. Gray admired both Browne's advice as a teacher and his contribution to poetry. Browne's one year as a teacher at the Iowa Workshop was followed by stints at Columbia University and Bennington College in Vermont. He arrived at the University of Minnesota in the fall of 1971. By then he had published his first collection of poems, *The Wife of Winter* (Scribners, 1970), which included some splendid poems he wrote while at Iowa and later on as well.

The Wife of Winter adumbrated Browne's greatest desire as a young poet, wanting to find a voice in the New Land where he had decided to stay rather than move back to England. Finding a mate, a partner in life, is the underlying theme throughout this first collection, although it is hinted at now and then, never directly imputed. In *Selected Poems 1965-1995*, the pity is that his first collection is so thinly represented. The reason may be in part that the earlier poems represented a youth and early manhood left far behind as the poet approached and went through the better part of middle age, adding more collections of poetry to his canon, and a solid marriage and the advent of three children to his domestic life, never far from his concerns as a poet. This is understandable, although much of the early Browne, with delightful poems such as "Three Songs" and "Losing WSUI" and "Iowa," is left back in the now out-of-print first book, to be discovered perhaps in a library which keeps such things or in a provident used bookstore. Before discussing what *is* represented in the new book, here is the third and final section of "Three Songs"; see if you don't hear the music that Darrell Gray spoke of so admiringly:

Playing tennis in the snow
With my true love, most gladly I

Did let her win each game, each set;
I praised her grave, inaccurate eye,

And proudly as she leapt the net
Did raise her in that world of snow

And sing the song all lovers know.
Six Love, Six Love, do such games go.

This poem was well-received when it first appeared in print more than thirty years ago. It still holds up well. Browne, who liked to enter a room wearing a greatcoat and black riding boots or some other adornment to gather attention, was well-regarded as a poet's poet, one who could make a poem sing as well as dance, who gave back the joy of poetry in the dark age of Vietnam, Lyndon Johnson's military draft and the brooding insistence that defending American interests abroad and at home meant young men should go off to Vietnam and risk death in a senseless war.

Yet if Browne sensed the lack of buoyant song in that age, despite Peter, Paul and Mary, Robert Bly, Eugene McCarthy and Allen Ginsberg leading the young as minstrels carrying poems and ballads and bells, if not the spirit, out of a dark age of body counts and drug overdoses, he could at least write about what he knew to be wrong and destructive. In this instance, Browne is direct and forceful, the cadences quick, the images unmistakable in their aggregate urgency and simplicity:

There are men making death together in the wood

We have not deserved this undergrowth
We have not merited this mud
O Jesus this mud

There are men making death together in the wood

My sergeant lies in a poisoned shadow
My friend has choked on a flower
The birds are incontinent in their terror . . .

They leave us over the hill
They are grass
They are dust
They are shed alone
Cold as the moon

And the widow moon above
Is cold and white
And will let no lovers in tonight
(from "The Delta")

Browne's early influences, certainly Dylan Thomas and Theodore Roethke as masters of rhythm within poetic cadence, pervade these early poems. Roethke's "Elegy for Jane" – about one of his students who was killed – is echoed strongly in Browne's lines:

Birds on the branch outside my window.
I wish they were Elie,
I wish they were Kate. . . .

I do not want you thrown
out of a car, your lives,
an evening in April, when I was driving
the same way, back, back here. . . .
(from "Elegy")

The pain is real and durable, so much so that reprinting the poem after a quarter century brings again the knowledge of arbitrary life and death so constantly renewed in the rush of current events. The lines are direct with deceptively simple imagery until the aggregate builds up, the elongations of emotion in a three-page poem.

Yet a poet must have means, if his ability to sing survives at all, to celebrate joy as well as pain and life's natural passages as well as death. Browne's ability to infuse his own longing for happiness, domestic happiness in this case, is reflected in a poem for two friends at their wedding, published in his second book, *The Sun Fetcher* (Carnegie-Mellon, 1978), and reprinted here. Incantation, surds of direct notion if not always complicated imagery, evoke again the strains of yearning implicit in *The Wife of Winter* and laid out starkly in "Epithalamion/Wedding Dawn"; here are four worthy sections:

Happy the man who is thirsty.
And the moths, pilgrims to our screens.

The fisher stands waist-deep in the water,
waiting. Happy the man waiting.

Who is not alone? Who does not sleep
in the dark house of himself, without music?
The world, a collapsed fire, shows only its smoke,
and the smoke hides its hills . . .

You must not be angry with this planet.
For we are in a company
whose music surpasses its pain.
For I tell you, I sat in the dark, also,
and the wedding light came onto my window . . .

The dawn that came up the day of your wedding
took me in its hand like the creature I am;
and I heard the dark that I came from
whispering "Be silent."
And the dawn said "Sing."
And I found the best words I could find around me,
and came to your wedding.

There is, again, the counterpoint of reality. If there is happiness and cause for celebration, for gaiety on occasion, it will be offset by inexplicable tragedy. In this vein, Browne's strategy effectively melds the imagery of a particular occasion with what is happening across the world in a place utterly hostile. Here is the entirety of "Hallowe'en 1971":

I carve my first head. Then I carve another.
Now I have two Vietnamese
children on my table.

I place a candle in each of them, & light it.
The heads are still wet inside. I've put
the seeds in a brown bag.

I take one head to the window.
The other I put on my stair, with the front
door open. By it, a bowl of candy.

Down the block,
round the neighborhood,

all over this darkened country,
the hollow yellow heads
burning in windows, & tiny
American ghosts running toward them
through the dark, with open hands.

Another poem on the opposite page celebrates the macabre in a different tone, that of allusion instead of direct statement about John Berryman's 1972 suicide by jumping off a bridge at the University of Minnesota. The motif of an owl suddenly visiting campus one day in late fall of that year but gone the next morning is poignant by inference only: "He is there, with his large eyes, / high above us, / who were never close. / He will not say, he will not say / what it is he wants. / But we are glad he is there, / we without wings. / There is nothing he need not do. / And if he jumps, / we need not fear for him." A brilliant evocation, this short poem does not mention death or dying, but is simply dedicated to Berryman.

There are other poems in different modes: the skillful, almost raucous, cadences in "Robert Bly Gets Up Early," the near-Buddhist luminations of "Sun Exercises" and the strains again of Roethke with suddenly remembered grief not there but the memory of it in "My Father's Music" – here are the beginning strophes:

For fourteen years I have not heard
that Bach prelude played for me as I sat
alone in the back of the church.
Fourteen years since my dear musician died.

And she plays my father's music now,
this woman in Minnesota.
Not his, I know now,
but the sounds he served
in the dark church . . .

Another element in Browne's poetic arsenal is found in "Robert Bly Gets Up Early," which I will not quote from here, but it is also rampant in "Fox" – near-riotous comedy of associations, incantatory images following each other in Blakean fashion like circus elephants, although in this case inspired when the poet happened to see a red fox while driving in rural Wisconsin. Originally published in *The New Yorker*, "Fox" accrues passing facts of the poet's life into a surreal fantasy. A three-and-a-half page poem, "Fox" moves swiftly:

The fox! It is a fox! It is a red fox!
I slow up. He is in the road.
I slow. He moves into the grass, but not far.
He doesn't seem that afraid.
Look, look! I saw to the white dog behind me.
Look, Snow Dog, a fox! He doesn't see him.
And this fox. What he does now is
go a little further, & turn, & look at me.
I am braked, with the engine running,
looking at him . . .

Be fox for all of us, those in zoos,
in classrooms, those on committees,
neither Assistant Fox nor Associate Fox
but Full Fox, fox with tenure, runner
on any land, owner of nothing, anywhere,
fox beyond all farmers,
fox neither Israeli nor Arab,
fox the color of the fall & the hill . . .

& the leaves falling, red, red.
And the fox runs on.

By the mid-1980s, Browne's next collection, *Smoke From The Fires* (Carnegie-Mellon, 1985), saw a sharpening of vision as the poet's private life had assumed the responsibilities of domesticity and the realization of birth and death as in a single instant for their staggering import. Browne's invocation of the beginning of life, as in "Lamb" – with its taut, excited lines – is as strong as the bucolic lament in the very next poem in the book, "Dream At The Death Of James Wright":

The wind is rolling the buffalo down;
the wind is shining and sharpening the buffalo
and rolling them down . . .
They don't know enough to
come together , bind their black fur
together, sit out the storm . . .

Again, the tremors of birth and death so closely aligned, as if the poet realizes they are inextricable, that what lies in between is a precious, fleeting time soon to be lost forever.

In 1992, Browne saw his fourth collection, *You Won't Remember This*, appear, and within its pages, reflections of the age which included a frenetic search for Joseph Mengele, the infamous Nazi doctor, culminating in an excavation of what was purported to be his grave. If poetry is anything, it is an examination of larger themes by blowing up details, not dissimilar to a film-maker's device of inserting fictional lives into a larger scenario and seeing how the characters interact, what their smaller story means within the larger whole. In "Mengele," the poet knows very well that Mengele lives in all of us, whether we like it or not, for his monstrosity was a minor theme within a much more barbarous epic. Here is the third and final strophe, executed in repeated striations of horror:

> Don't bother showing me pictures
> of the remains of Mengele,
> the remains are alive and well
> and simmering in our rivers
> or climbing into our houses out of the ground
> where they will not be confined
> or sliding inside the rain
> out of the summer air, oh yes,
> the remains are even there, I tell you,
> are alive and well, are everywhere.

By this time, the poet had passed fifty, had long since been granted tenure and a full professorship, and his children were growing up fast. His father had died many years earlier, but in this later period, his mother dies, and in lines from "A Wild and Calm Lament for My Mother," Browne takes risks of sentiment to a more bulbous stage. But these are real emotions, fused with his own children and their care: "These lambs about me, their leaping, / the wife I am learning continually / to love, if I cannot / name these amazements daily, / how am I your son? The days / ease into another summer, / old branches recover their green, / and these faces, in whom I see you, / lean, oh, eagerly, toward the world . . . " This poem is followed immediately by several poems about parenthood, the notions simple and declared as such where the poet and his wife entertain their small son – "Dancing For Him":

> He likes to watch us dance, we do it
> for him, he laughs, we waltz
> around him in the kitchen or polka,
> leaping, through the living room, he
> laughs, or cheek to cheek like

a dragged-out marathon couple we
slouch and stagger, he throws back
his months' old head and laughs.

What he'll remember of these times,
who knows? Maybe one morning,
walking from a dream of faces,
he'll turn to one beside him, saying:
"That's it! They used to dance for me!"

The title poem in the fourth collection, reprinted here, is about the birth of his younger daughter and her first tentative days. The poem has the veins of memory within its sinews, as Browne recalls his past in England, his parents when he was a small child, as his daughter is small, that she "won't remember" moments when her parents caught her fragility in their memories, as the poet/father remembers his own early years:

Cresting the stony hill, the edge of England,
        and there was the sea,
the holiday town our parents brought us to
        when I was fourteen.
I found the dunes where we'd tumbled,
        swam in those waves again,
the breakers forever rolling in
        from the new world.

Such a boy I was then, all aware
        of myself in the waves;
but now the salted element itself
        and look, so many the swimmers . . .

The final section of *Selected Poems 1965-1995* has a few "new" poems, more evocations of the poet's father, gone over thirty years:

Saying goodnight last night
to my boy, I could hear you;
carrying my dreaming girl
to her proper bed, I remembered
your own pale body
our final summer,
the veins blue as rivers
as you led us to water.

Wherever the son
may travel, let there be
doors without any number
where the father may enter.
(from "On The Anniversary")

In another smaller effort, the poet imbibes the dubious odors of political correctness. Whether he believes what he is saying is not the point, of course. The fact that he has said it will pacify the strident in academic committee meetings, appeasing reality in the face of luminous eyes and ears, these terse lines with the barest imagery:

Darkness is falling

That microphone clipped
To his lapel

Could be a twig to a stick beetle
or even a snail.

Were this not a senate hearing
But the forest floor

Something is crawling
("I Believe Anita Hill")

In sum, then, what can be said of the journey Michael Dennis Browne has taken as a poet? He writes poetry and teaches, refrains from writing literary criticism if at all possible and has never had to starve in a garret for the sake of his craft. He has had a life of comfort, what one would expect of an academic poet who nonetheless writes as if he were a thousand miles away from a classroom. A few grants have come his way, sabbaticals of course. His course as a poet is to repeat certain themes as life repeats them. But the variances are always new, unexpected. Such quirks make his craftsmanship weave fresh instances in a life where much has been given. *Selected Poems 1965-1995*, while not faithful entirely to his early work by dint of omission, nonetheless provides a worthy clue of his accomplishment since then. It is not without example for those who might study or practice this perilous art.

JAMES NAIDEN

OBSEQUIOUSNESS AS AN ART

YOU'RE TOO KIND *A Brief History Of Flattery*, by Richard Stengel (Simon & Schuster, 2000, 315 pp., New York; cloth, $25).

This book is in large format, over 300 pages including notes and acknowledgments. In other words, at almost 400 words a page, it would be a thick tome in a regular format. The plan is that of a college course in Western Civilization. Stengel's text begins with Egypt, makes a short stop with Israel, then Greece, Rome, the Middle Ages, later Italy, France, England, America and the modern United States. There is no room for China, Japan, India or the Zulus, but there is an anticipatory chapter on simian grooming behavior, which Stengel thinks is a parallel or analogy to flattery.

The tone darkens as the book progresses. It is clear that Stengel is offended by current locutions that he thinks overdone, however transparent their insincerity may be. In Hollywood and New York, he sees the main offenders. He quotes original languages but not always to good effect. In a chapter on Greece, he misspells a key word, *parresia*, which he repeatedly spells *parhesia*. Not everyone knows Greek, of course, but this reviewer does, so for him this display of pretended learning falls flat.

It is salutory to turn to a passage that makes the author shine – that on Lord Chesterton will do well. His humanity and kindness warm our hearts. Dale Carnegie, on the other hand, merits only contempt from Stengel. *How to Win Friends and Influence People* merits no laudation. I had a better opinion of Carnegie. The media have reported a story from Japan that makes clear the value of what Carnegie did, however mediocre his motivation. Apparently in Japan the custom is not to give compliments. Two enterprising young businessmen have offered to give compliments to customers for a price. 'I know they are doing it for money but I like it anyway,' said one satisfied customer.

What disturbs Stengel most is the introduction into the American persona of the quality which he terms personality, for which intrusion he assigns blame to Carnegie. As Stengel defines it, personality is a baneful and artificial distortion of outward behavior, opposed to the action that comes from the inspiration of better impulses and traditional mores. There exist people for whom the term is free from such opprobrium, who have not read Carnegie and have thought he was merely advising them to be pleasant.

Apart from such cavils, this book is well written and embellished by many witty remarks.

J. R. NAIDEN

Brief Mentions . . . .

Shadow Baby, by Alison McGhee (Harmony Books/Random House, New York, 2000, 243 pp.; cloth, $23).

This is Alison McGhee's second novel since 1998. Her first, *Rainlight*, was textured and influenced by the atmosphere she had grown up with in Sterns, New York, a community in the Adirondack Mountain area. Sterns is the *mise-én-scene* of much of McGhee's fiction. This new novel is a kind of extension of her first one in that some of the same characters reappear, although the major characters linger in one's mind long after one has finished the book. There is Clara winter, age 11, who insists on spelling her last name with a small 'w' because she was born during a snowstorm in a vehicle that had slid into a ditch; her twin sister did not survive. Her one friend is a 77-year-old retired metal-worker, Georg Kominsky, an immigrant from a European country that no longer exists. She interviews him for an oral-history project she has taken on, if anything, because her school-age peers are not up to her level of precocity.

From the old man, Clara learns to look for salvageable metal objects and forge them into useful items. One day Georg drives her to Utica to visit her maternal grandfather whom she had never seen before. The grandfather is virtually speechless at her unannounced visit, but later he arrives in Sterns and answers some of her persistent questions. Her mother Tamar had conceived after being raped by a man whose name she never knew, and Clara's questions are unremitting. Tamar bears them with as much monosyllabic grace as she can. One night there is a fire in the old man's trailer. Clara enters the trailer, thinking the old man might be trapped. In fact, he had been to the grocery store and rushes into the trailer, tosses Clara out through a window but dies in the fire. The novel's title comes from the girl's determination to find out about her lost sister, whose name, her grandfather reveals, was Daphne.

There is much poetry within McGhee's prose in the way she depicts characters: the intelligent point-of-view from Clara's perspective, the humility of Georg, the old man, who – Clara discovers – does not know how to read, the ability of people in humble circumstances to live and not be bitter.

This book has already received much praise from critics throughout the United States. After reading it, I can only add that the story is well-told and realistic, the characters are believable and the language is direct yet poetic and lyrical. Alison McGhee has written a superb novel.

Mayflies New Poems and Translations, by Richard Wilbur (Harcourt, New York, 2000, 80 pp.; cloth, $22).

Richard Wilbur has been recognized as a significant American poet for over half a century. His disciplined, formal prosody seems effortless as he has moved from poem to poem, topic to topic, over the span of a long career. He was born in 1921.

This collection has both new poems and some translations – from the French of Mallarmé, Baudelaire and Moliére, the Romanian of Nina Cassian, the Bulgarian of Valeri Petrov, and the Italian of Dante Alighieri. For example, here is the entirety of Petrov's "A Cry From Childhood:

> Why must it come just now to trouble me,
> This sudden, shrill, and dreamlike cry
> Of children calling "Valeri! Valeri!"
> Out in the street nearby.
>
> It is not for me, that distant childhood call;
> Alas, it is for me no more.
> They care calling now to someone else, my small
> Namesake who lives next door.
>
> Though such disturbances, I must admit,
> Are troubling to my train of thought,
> I keep my feelings to myself, for it
> Would be comical, would it not,
>
> If, from his high and studious retreat,
> A gaunt old man leaned out to say
> "I can't come out" to the children in the street,
> "I'm not allowed to play."

Wilbur's own poetry is deftly resonant. In the title poem he watches a swarm of insects in a forest; here is the third and final strophe:

> Watching those lifelong dancers of a day
> As night closed in, I felt myself alone
>   In a life too much my own,
> More mortal in my separateness than they –
> Unless, I thought, I had been called to be
>   Not fly or star
> But one whose task is joyfully to see
> How fair the fiats of the caller are.

Then there is the beauty of Wilbur's technical skill, as in the sonnet "A Barred Owl":

> The warping night air having brought the boom
> Of an owl's voice into her darkened room,
> We tell the wakened child that all she heard
> Was an odd question from a forest bird,
> Asking of us, if rightly listened to,
> "Who cooks for you?" and then "Who cooks for you?"
>
> Words, which can make our terrors bravely clear,
> Can also thus domesticate a fear.
> And send a small child back to sleep at night
> Not listening for the sound of stealthy flight
> Or dreaming of some small thing in a claw
> Borne up to some dark branch and eaten raw.

Richard Wilbur is a major poet for at least two very good reasons: his high mastery of craft and the wide variety of subject matter throughout his *oeuvre*. This book is testament to a master at work.

Yesterday Had A Man In It, poems by Leslie Adrienne Miller (Carnegie-Mellon University Press, Pittsburgh, PA, 1998, 88 pp.; paper, $12).

Leslie Adrienne Miller is a very verbal poet who displays great energy – Robert Bly once called this kind of energy "breathing out" – although this is not a bad thing. Miller brings a first-rate education, high ambition and acute observation at every turn to her craft. For what this means, one can merely look at her three books published during the 1990s by Carnegie-Mellon. (Dina Ben-Lev reviews Miller's second collection elsewhere in this issue.) If you read this poet, be prepared to travel. You will go back in time to the Ohio of her youth and to other places she has been – Germany, Indonesia, Bali, south Texas, Maryland and not in the least the Twin Cities, where she teaches English at the University of St. Thomas.

At her best, Miller is crisp and pungent in her images. Her observational powers are always acute and sharp, as in these opening lines of the title poem:

> How many times might it happen
> in one woman's life that a man,
> a surprisingly bright and nice-looking man,
> gives her the gift of a day in the country –

> preferably a foreign country – and shows her
> something – an animal, a church, a cave,
> something about which he has a story?
> Often there are remarkable flowers involved,
> rain keeps to itself, and many more
> colors of green are discovered
> than anyone believed there could be . . .

Miller writes about former lovers or potential lovers with the same dispassionate verbosity that she discusses socks, warts, her parents, foreign cities or childhood memories. Anything is grist for a poem, as it should be. Here are the opening and final lines of "The Suit":

> In all honesty, I don't recall your tie,
> only that there was some flash under the fine
> black dress coat, its lapels so costly
> they lay steamed and obedient
> as airbrushed women. Are your feet
> beautiful? Is your mother alive? . . .
>
> Where did you get that suit? Who is that
> suit? Where does it live? How do you keep
> it so fine all day? How are, who are,
> when can we, should we, why do they, where
> are your real hands?

Leslie Adrienne Miller's output is impressive. The back cover of this book touts her professional credentials, two laudatory blurbs and a headshot in which the poet looks as if she might have just swallowed a goldfish. When she is writing tersely, not densely, she is at her best form. This is a highly credible collection of poems from one whose energy is unstoppable. You may learn more than a few things by reading this book cover to cover.

The Lynchings in Duluth, by Michael Fedo. Forward by William D. Green. (Minnesota Historical Society Press, 2000, new edition, Saint Paul, MN, 192 pp.; paper, $15).

This is a well-written, stark account of a little-remembered event in Minnesota history, the lynching of three young black men from a traveling circus who were thought to have raped a young white woman when in fact there was no solid evidence that this was true. Rumor and whipped-up emotions on a June night in 1920 led to a mob of men storming the understaffed Duluth city jail and dragging out three black men and hanging them from a light pole. Fedo, whose book was originally published in 1979, has updated the text and provided an account as disturbing as it is a reminder that mobs do ugly things, whether abetted by alcohol or not. In this case, the prevalent fear was a deeply imbedded racism of the times. When I read this book, the footage of young men harassing, groping, disrobing and taunting women in and around Central Park, New York City, was fresh news. The mentality is the same: the debasing of human life, treating other people as if their humanity counts for nothing, tearing their dignity into shreds while emotion and unreason prevail in a mob mentality. Fedo's book is a vivid reminder that such things happen anywhere, and – dare I say – at any time. That the 1920 lynchings happened in June, as did the events in Central Park eighty years later, makes one wonder if the sultry season adds to lack of rational thinking. Fedo writes clear, unadorned sentences and lets the evidence speak for itself. That legal recriminations were mild (only a very few went to jail as a result of the lynchings, and one black man was wrongly convicted of the rape and sent to prison) added to the tragedy. Fedo gives an account of the main figures in Duluth that evening and what happened to them later. The three lynched black men were buried in unmarked graves at first, then later their graves were identified.

This is a fine, if very disconcerting, book. Michael Fedo has done an invaluable service by writing it – and the Minnesota Historical Society Press has properly recognized his efforts by reprinting the book in a handsome paperback edition with a sobering black-and-white cover depicting members of the lynch mob standing next to the corpses of the three black men whose only "crime" was that they were in the wrong place at the wrong time. William D. Green, a historian at Augsburg College, provides a thoughtful Forward in this new edition from an African-American perspective.

The Natural Father, short stories by Robert Lacy (New Rivers Press, Minneapolis, MN, 1997, 219 pp.; paper, $14.95).

This first collection by a native Texan and U. S. Marine Corps veteran harkens back to those experiences, as well as a failed marriage, an uncertain college teaching career, and a stint working for a politician. Lacy evokes his past with forceful, direct narrative and pungent dialogue. The title story tells of a young Marine forty years ago who impregnates a young Jewish woman, sends her money for her postpartum stay in Arizona but never sees her again nor does he ever see their child. Butters is Lacy's protagonist, as he is in several stories. The ending is poignant: "When he was finished with the letter Butters set it beside him on the bunk, carefully, and picked up the release. It was short, too, just a single legal-sized page. It asked him to understand what he was doing – waiving all rights and responsibilities in the care and upbringing of the child – and it cited the pertinent sections of Arizona law, which took up most of the rest of the page. Toward the bottom, however, there was a dotted line that caught Butters' eye. He skipped over much of the legal language, but he lingered at the dotted line. 'Signature of Natural Father,' it was labeled. He looked at it. That was him. He was the natural father. He turned the page over to see if there was anything on the back. There wasn't. It was blank. He turned it back over and looked at the dotted line. Tipton was standing just a few feet away from him, waiting. They had already called their taxi. It was on the way.

"He looked up at Tipton. 'You got a pen?' he said."

Another of these stories – "The Buddy Floyd Story" – appeared in issue 10 of this publication nine years ago. It is a toughly-hewn, moving depiction of a young couple's marital problems mostly to do with lack of money, then a brief chance at redemption, a perfervid elation borne of alcohol and sentimentality for an irretrievable past, and an optimistic though guarded denouement. Robert Lacy has produced a superb collection, well worth reading and having in one's library of good fiction. The book has an attractive cover and is reasonably priced.

Far From Russia A Memoir, by Olga Andreyev Carlisle (St. Martin's Press, New York, 2000, 182 pp.; cloth, $22.95).

This is the fourth non-fiction book Olga Andreyev Carlisle has written about life in Russia and elsewhere. She published her first book, *Voices In The Snow*, nearly forty years ago about her first visit to the then Soviet Union when she had an assignment from *The Paris Review* to bring back an interview with Nobel Laureate Boris Pasternak. Andreyev Carlisle, the daughter of Russian expatriates who opposed the Bolsheviks before they left their homeland, was born in Paris more than a decade after Lenin and his revolutionaries seized power. This new book, then, tells the story (as the three previous books did not) of her Paris upbringing, her Russian parents, her education in both France and later in the United States, and how she met and fell in love with a young American, Henry Carlisle, in the post-war France of half a century ago. She depicts their courtship, their friends from many places, their wedding in Paris, the birth of their son Michael, then eventually moving to the United States, and life among artists and writers both on Nantucket and in New York City. Passing through her narrative are Robert Motherwell, Senator Robert F. Kennedy, Norman Mailer, Lillian Hellman, Blair Clark, Allen Ginsberg, Fay Lansner, Alexander Solzhenitsyn and at the very end a recapitulation of her first meeting in Peredelkino with Pasternak, who had known her parents and gave her a warm welcome.

While Andreyev Carlisle writes in a smooth, painterly style, I discovered numerous comma splices as well as two typos early in the narrative. More rigorous editing would have pruned these out from an otherwise admirable book, which will appeal to writers, artists, Russophiles and anyone interested in knowing what a cultivated, tri-lingual observer of life in and outside Russia has experienced.

JAMES NAIDEN

NOTES ON CONTRIBUTORS

CHESTER G. ANDERSON contributed some poems to our previous issue. A poem sequence, a short story and a book review were published in earlier issues. He now lives with his wife Carole in Mount Dora, Florida. He is Professor Emeritus of English at the University of Minnesota.

REBECCA ARONSON teaches poetry and composition at the University of New Mexico, where she is currently a visiting lecturer. Her poetry has appeared recently in *Alligator Jumper*, *Hayden's Ferry Review* and on buses throughout New Mexico as a part of *Ride The Moon*, the New Mexico Vehicle Project. Ms. Aronson is a native of Minneapolis.

JAMES ASHE, a native of Ireland, is a physician engaged in research about brain and motor functions. In our previous issue, he contributed a review-article about the prose of William Trevor. He lives in North Oaks, Minnesota.

ALLEN HAMILTON BATES is, among his many professional accomplishments, an actor, director, and voice-over in the Twin Cities. He lives with his wife Camille in Minneapolis.

ROBERT BATTIN has contributed art work here before. He is also a printmaker and letter press printer. He lives with his wife Uta in Minneapolis.

MARVIN BELL has a long list of books to his credit, among them the two from 1994 that Carol Ellis discusses here. In our next issue, Ms. Ellis will have a conversation with Mr. Bell, and we will print more of his recent poems to accompany the interview. Mr. Bell teaches at the Iowa Writers' Workshop part of each academic year in Iowa City, where he lives with his wife, Dorothy. They also live part of the year in Port Townsend, Washington. In March 2000, Mr. Bell was named Iowa's first Poet Laureate. In September 2000, his new book, *Nightworks: Poems 1962-2000*, appeared from Copper Canyon Press.

DINA BEN-LEV lives and teaches in Cincinnati. Her volume of poems, *Broken Helix*, appeared from Mid-List Books in 1997.

SIGRID BERGIE had a book of poems, *Turning Out The Lights*, published by New Rivers Press in 1988. The volume received favorable reviews;

Beverly Mand discussed it in our tenth issue in late 1991. Ms. Bergie also works as a Poet-In-The-Schools in Minnesota. She lives in Minneapolis.

KEVIN BEZNER now lives in Charlotte, North Carolina, although he submitted his poem a while back from Missoula, Montana.

ROBERT BLY's most recent book of prose, *The Sibling Society*, is discussed in these pages by Camille D'Ambrose. Mr. Bly lives with his wife Ruth in Minneapolis, although they also spend time at a second home in Moose Lake, Minnesota.

JULIA BUDENZ lives in Cambridge, Massachusetts, and also spends time in Rome, Italy. She is writing a poem in five books, "The Gardens of Flora Baum," begun in 1970. The conclusion of the second book was published as a separate volume, *From the Gardens of Flora Baum* (Wesleyan University Press, 1984). Other sections have appeared in American and British journals.

MARJORIE BUETTNER lives with her husband Gregory and three daughters in Minneapolis. She has published in *North Coast Review*, *Loonfeather*, *Sidewalks*, and other journals, both print and on-line.

RICHARD CARR graduated a while back from Macalester College. When last heard from, he was teaching in the English Department at Bowling Green University, in Ohio.

JARED CARTER's two books of poems are *Work, for the Night Is Coming* (Macmillan, 1981) and *After The Rain* (Cleveland State University Poetry Center, 1982). He lives in Indianapolis.

BARRY CASSELMAN has published in a number of journals since he graduated from the Iowa Writers' Workshop, including *The American Poetry Review* and *Another Chicago Magazine*. He is also a journalist, specializing in politics. A native of Erie, Pennsylvania, he has lived for some time now in Minneapolis.

CLARK COOLIDGE has lived in western Massachusetts since 1970. In 1968, some of his poems appeared in Paul Carroll's famous anthology, *The Young American Poets* (Big Table, Chicago). His recent books are *Keys To The Caverns* (Zasterle Press, 1995) and *For Kurt Cobain* (The Figures, 1995).

CHET COREY lives in Bloomington, Minnesota. He teaches at Normandale Community College. His poetry has appeared in *Chiron Review, Fresh Ground, Rag Mag* and *Sidewalks*. He is a former editor of *The Great River Review*.

ROBERT COUTEAU is a writer who lives in Paris, France.

DAVID CULVER is a Twin Cities artist who prefers to work with stone. His drawings have appeared in previous issues of this publication.

CAMILLE D'AMBROSE is a writer, actress and director who has been associated with many theaters around the country. She holds a Master's degree in Liberal Studies from Hamline University, in Saint Paul. Ms. D'Ambrose lives with her husband Allen Hamilton Bates in Minneapolis.

JOHN DANIEL has contributed poems and critical prose to these pages for many years. He earned his Ph.D. in English from the University of Minnesota back in 1973. He lives in Plymouth, England, where he recently retired from Plymouth University.

KATE HALLETT DAYTON is a writer living in the Twin Cities. Her work has appeared in *Iowa Woman, Hungry Mind Review*, and *Minnesota Monthly*, among other places. She teaches at The Loft and at Normandale Community College.

CHARLES EDWARD EATON's recent book of poems, *The Country of the Blue*, is reviewed here by Richard Holinger. Mr. Eaton lives in Chapel Hill, North Carolina.

CAROL ELLIS is both a poet and a prolific writer on American poetry. Her recent work has appeared in *The Nebraska Review* and *Mediphors*, among other places. She has done extensive interviews with Marvin Bell and Charles Wright, and has written on other poets, including John Berryman and James Wright. In our next issue, Ms. Ellis will have an extended, updated interview with Marvin Bell. She lives in Redlands, California.

DAVE ETTER has published several books of poetry, including *Sunflower* (Spoon River Press, Box 6, Granite Falls, Minnesota, 56241; 1994) and *How High the Moon* (also Spoon River, 1996). He lives in Elburn, Illinois.

MICHAEL FEDO is an author *of the Lynchings in Duluth* (Minnesota Historical Society Press, Saint Paul, MN, 2000), discussed in our "Brief Mentions" section in this issue. He has published short stories in *The North American Review*, *AmericanWay* and other journals. Mr. Fedo lives in Coon Rapids, Minnesota.

ROLAND FLINT is retired from the English Department of Georgetown University. He has published widely over many years. His book, *Selected Poems 1965-1982*, appeared from Dial in 1983. He lives in Silver Spring, Maryland.

CALVIN FORBES has a pair of books out, *Blue Monday* (Wesleyan University Press, 1974) and *From The Book of Shine* (Burning Deck, 1979). He teaches at The School of The Art Institute of Chicago, and lives in that city.

HUGH FOX teaches English at Michigan State University. He lives in East Lansing.

NANCY FREDERICKSEN had work in our previous issue in 1995. She works as a legal secretary in Minneapolis and lives in nearby Coon Rapids.

DANIELA GIOSEFFI lives in Andover, New Jersey. Her most recent book is *On Prejudice* (Doubleday, 1993).

EAMON GRENNAN, a native of Ireland, teaches English at Vassar College in Poughkeepsie, New York. His recent volume, *So It Goes*, is available from Graywolf Press.

NICKIE J. GUNSTROM lives in Reno, Nevada. Her poems have most recently appeared in *The Midwest Quarterly*, *Northern Contours* and *The Dickinson Review*.

KARLA HAMMOND is a well-published writer living in East Hampton, Connecticut.

WILLIAM HATHAWAY lives in Southampton, New York. His latest collection of poems, *Sightseeer* (Canio's Editons, Box 552, Sagaponack, NY 11962), was published in 2000.

ARCHIBALD HENDERSON lives in Houston, Texas. His poems have appeared here twice before. His most recent volume is *Where You Are Now* (Latitudes Press, Mansfield, TX, 1984).

WILLIAM HEYEN's most recent collection, *Crazy Horse In Stillness* (BOA Editions, Brockport, NY, 1994), is reviewed here by Richard Holinger. Mr. Heyen lives and teaches in Brockport.

TIMOTHY HODOR was born in East Chicago, Indiana, in 1953. His chapbook, *Hours in Orchestration*, was published by Monte Verita in 1984. He now lives in Vienna, Austria.

RICHARD HOLINGER's reviews have appeared here before. He lives in Geneva, Illinois.

DAVID IGNATOW taught in the Creative Writing Graduate Program at Columbia University, although he lived in East Hampton, Long Island. His recent book, *I Have A Name*, appeared in September 1996 from Wesleyan University Press. Several of the poems here are in the collection. Mr. Ignatow died 19 November 1997 at age 83.

DONALD JUNKINS spent a good amount of time not long ago in China, the source of these new poems. Mr. Junkins has several books to his credit. He teaches in the Creative Writing Graduate Program at the University of Massachusetts, Amherst.

KATHRYN KRISHNA submitted these poems a long time ago from Montana, and we have since lost contact with her. Under another name, she was a student in the Iowa Writers Workshop back in the late 1960s. Where are you, Kathryn?

ROBERT LACY's collection of short stories, *The Natural Father*, appeared from New Rivers Press in the spring of 1997. He has published many short stories in the last decade or so, including two in previous issues of this publication. A native of Texas, he is also a graduate of the University of Iowa Writers Workshop (1966) and now lives with his wife Susan in Medicine Lake, Minnesota.

LEE LARCOMB is another writer we've lost contact with completely. We know that he was a friend of the late Darrell Gray (1945-1986), but we can find no record of where the poet was when he sent his work to us or where he is now. Alas.

JAMES LONGSTAFF has published poems here before. A former resident of Minnesota, he and his wife Patricia now live near Cazenovia in upstate New York. He is also a fiction writer.

GLENNA LUSCHEI edits Solo Press in San Luis Obispo, California. She has several books to her credit, among them *Pianos Around the Cape* (Asperont Press, San Francisco, 1999), reviewed in our "Brief Mentions" section.

RICHARD LYONS retired a while back from the English Department at North Dakota State University. His most recent book is *Enough To Be A Woman* (Scopecraeft Press, 1992). He now lives in Gardiner, Maine.

CLARENCE MAJOR has published numerous books of poetry and fiction over the years. He is currently Professor of English at University of California-Davis.

GERARD MALANGA lives in New York City. His most recent volume of poems is *Mythologies of the Heart* (Black Sparrow Press, Santa Rose, CA, 1996).

FREYA MANFRED lives with her husband, Tom Pope, a screenwriter, and their two sons in Shorewood, Minnesota. She has published three books of poetry, among them *American Roads* (Overlook, 1980).

ALISON McGHEE writes both poetry and fiction. Her most recent novel, *Shadow Baby* (Harmony Books, 2000), is discussed in our "Brief Mentions" section. She teaches Creative Writing at Metropolitan State University in Saint Paul.

SUSAN McLEAN lives alternately in Marshall, Minnesota, where she teaches English at Southwest State University, and Iowa City, Iowa. She has published her work also in *Kalliope, Hurricane Alice* and *The Wolf Head Quarterly*.

LESLIE ADRIENNE MILLER teaches English at the University of Saint Thomas in Saint Paul, where she lives. Her second collection of poems,

Ungodliness (Carnegie-Mellon, 1994), is reviewed here by Dina Ben-Lev. Her third collection, *Yesterday Had A Man In It*, was released by Carnegie-Mellon in the spring of 1998 and is discussed in our "Brief Mentions" section.

RALPH J. MILLS, JR., first made his mark back in the 1960s as a literary critic and editor, then became a widely published poet. He now has a good number of books, both prose and poetry, to his credit. A collection of poems, *Sky Swept*, appeared in the spring of 1997 and is reviewed here by John Daniel. Mr. Mills lives in Chicago, where he is now retired from the English Department at the University of Illinois-Chicago Circle.

JOHN MITCHELL has been a contributor to these pages since 1972. He lives with his wife Jean in Minneapolis and teaches English at Augsburg College.

MICHAEL MOOS has published three books, including *A Long Way To See* (North Dakota Institute for Regional Studies, 1987). His work has appeared in five anthologies and he has received several fellowships and awards. He lives in Saint Paul, Minnesota.

W. R. MOSES is long retired from the English Department of Kansas State University. He has published six collections of poetry over the years, including *Passage* (Wesleyan University Press, 1976) and *Not Native* (Juniper Press, La Cross, WI, 1979). Mr. Moses lives in Manhattan, Kansas.

JAMES NAIDEN has published poetry and literary criticism for nearly four decades, most recently in *The Wolf Head Quarterly, The Widener Review* and *The New Hibernia Review*. He has lived in Minneapolis since 1970.

J. R. NAIDEN had a long academic career at a good number of colleges and universities before retiring from full-time teaching in 1978. He lives in Seattle.

CHARLOTTE OTTEN is Professor of English at Calvin College, Grand Rapids, Michigan. She has published her work widely and has edited an anthology of poems about child-bearing.

JOE PADDOCK has published several books of poems over the years, including *Boar's Dance* (Holy Cow Press, Duluth, 1993; $8.95, paper). He lives with his wife Nancy in Litchfield, Minnesota.

NILS PETERSON published a collection of poems, *The Comedy of Desire*, in 1993. He teaches Shakespeare and Creative Writing at San Jose State University. The Editors are grateful to Robert Bly for making us aware of Mr. Peterson's poem.

MARY POGGE graduated a while back from Nebraska Wesleyan University with a Bachelor's degree in English. She is now raising a daughter, teaching Korean martial art and living in Pinckney, Michigan. She writes both poetry and fiction.

PAUL RAMSEY, who died in September 1994 at age 69, was Poet-In-Residence and Distinguished Alumni Professor of English at the University of Tennessee-Chattanooga. His works included seven volumes of poetry and books of scholarship and criticism, among them *The Art of John Dryden*, as well as many scholarly articles.

ROBIN RAYGOR has published both poetry and fiction over the years. He lives with his family in Saint Paul.

JOHN CALVIN REZMERSKI is Writer-in-Residence at Gustavus Adolphus College in St. Peter, Minnesota. A while back, he edited *A Frederick Manfred Reader* (Holy Cow! Press, Duluth, MN, 1996). In 2000, Mr. Rezmerski's new collection of poems, *What Do I Know? New And Selected Poems*, was published by Holy Cow Press and is reviewed here by Marjorie Buettner. Mr. Rezmerski lives in Eagle Lake, Minnesota.

GEORGE ROBERTS has taught English in the Minneapolis Public School System for many years. He has three books of poems to his credit. His prose poems here reflect his teaching experiences. Of these prose poems, to be collected in a book entitled *Elfriede's Cat*, he writes: "I am attentive not to give too much away. . . . resist the urge to type them up too soon. For this and other reasons, I stand breathing faint clouds of fog onto the cold pane of the hall window. Three inches of new snow have fallen during the night and I am not yet ready to ask what it has covered. The street light in the alley plants a shadow inside each footprint left along our sidewalk path by Elfriede's cat. Some hidden gesture of night nudges my glance upward – into winter trees, dark and tangled, like maps of the circulatory system pinned to the wall of the gray-blue sky. My best lesson plans wander outside there with the cat. I have no reason to call them in."

MARC J. SHEEHAN submitted his poem from Grand Rapids, Michigan.

SAUDAMINI SIEGRIST teaches American literature at St. John's University, Queens, New York. She is also a student of meditation teacher Sri Chinmoy. She lives in Jamaica, New York.

JONATHAN SISSON and his wife Linda returned to his native Boston in 1995 after nearly thirty years on and off in Minnesota. He is a graduate of both Harvard University and the University of Minnesota. He has published poems, fiction and literary criticism for a long time in many publications. His chapbook of poems, *Where Silkwood Walks*, appeared from The Lake Street Review Press in 1981 and was favorably reviewed by Steven Eide in our revival issue, Number #9, in 1990.

THOMAS R. SMITH has published four books of poetry, among them *The Lost Music* (The Bookpress, Rivers Falls, WI, 1996), reviewed here by John Daniel. His most recent volume, *The Dark Indigo Current* (Holy Cow Press, 2000), is reviewed here by Marjorie Buettner. Mr. Smith now lives in Rivers Falls after spending a number of years in the Twin Cities.

JANE SPIRO had poetry in our previous issue. She is an educator and lives in Plymouth, England.

MADELON SPRENGNETHER has published volumes of both poetry and prose, most recently a book about Sigmund Freud. She is Professor of English at the University of Minnesota.

RUTH STONE's recent book of poems, *Simplicity* (Paris Press, Box 267, Northampton, MA 01061-0267), is reviewed here by John Daniel. She lives in Brandon, Vermont, and teaches during the academic year at SUNY-Binghamton, New York.

ROBERT JOE STOUT writes free-lance for a variety of magazines, including *Ruralite, Notre Dame Magazine, Penthouse* and *Army Magazine*. His most recent book is *They Still Play Baseball The Old Way* (Coffee Store Press, 1994). He divides his time between his home in Chico, California, and La Paz, Mexico.

STEVEN STROMME lives with his family in Avon, Minnesota. His work has appeared in *Modern Haiku, Lower Stumpf Lake Review, Sidewalks* and *Upper Mississippi Harvest.*

STEVEN TARLOW lives in Teaneck, New Jersey, where he is employed as a software engineer. He also has poems published in *Northwest Review* and *Paterson Literary Review*.

JEAN VALENTINE has published in leading journals for a long time and seen a number of books published. Her most recent volume, *Growing Darkness, Growing Light*, reviewed here by John Daniel, appeared in 1997 from Carnegie-Mellon. Her poem in this issue appears in that collection. Ms. Valentine won the Yale Series of Younger Poets Award back in 1965 with her first volume, *Dream Barker*. She now lives alternately in New York City and County Sligo, Ireland.

LOUISE VISTE-ROSS contributed drawings and lines to a collaborative poem in our last issue. A graduate of the University of Minnesota, she lives with her husband Nathan in Minneapolis.

NATHAN VISTE-ROSS had a poem sequence – "Cubes" – in our twelfth issue back in 1995. He lives with Louise in Minneapolis.

PHILIP WATERHOUSE lives in Bakersfield, California.

SUSAN WELLS is active in poetry circles in the Los Angeles area.

JANE WHITLEDGE lives in Winton, Minnesota. She has published her poems in *Yankee* and *The Widener Review*, among other places.

DARA WIER has four books of poems available. She lives in Amherst, Massachusetts.

BARON WORMSER is a librarian who lives Mercer, Maine. His book, *Atoms, Soul Music and Other Poems* appeared from Paris Review Editions in 1989. His more recent volume is *When* (Sarabande Books, Louisville, KY, 1997).

GEORGE T. WRIGHT lives in Tucson, Arizona. His book of poems, *Aimless Life*, appeared in 1999 from North Stone Editions and is reviewed here by Marjorie Buettner. He retired from the English Department at the University of Minnesota at the end of 1993.

TRACY YOUNGBLOM lives in Minneapolis with her three sons. Her work has appeared in several periodicals, including *Shenandoah, Kansas Quarterly,* and *Loonfeather*.

SUSAN YUZNA was a 1995 Bush Fellow in Poetry. Her first book of poems, *Her Slender Dress* (Akron, 1996), is reviewed here by John Daniel. At last report, she was living in the Twin Cities.